Carys Hughes 2G
History of the Mary Erskine School

A Family Unbroken

A Family Unbroken

1694-1994

THE MARY ERSKINE SCHOOL
TERCENTENARY HISTORY

LYDIA SKINNER

Photography by Philip Hyne

THE MARY ERSKINE SCHOOL
1994

Produced for The Mary Erskine School by
JohnTuckwell
The Mill House, Phantassie, East Linton,
East Lothian EH40 3DG, Scotland

ISBN 1 898410 60 7 (hardback)
ISBN 1 898410 61 5 (paperback)

Designed by Almond Design · Edinburgh
Printed and Bound by
Redwood Books,
Trowbridge, Wiltshire

CONTENTS

FOREWORD

This new work by Lydia Skinner is an important update on the history of The Mary Erskine School. Her work was commissioned to coincide with the celebration of the Tercentenary of the foundation. Her careful researches cover the whole history, but focus on the period from 1870 to the present day, a period which has seen many crises addressed and a continuing development of the campus and the curriculum.

The Merchant Company are delighted to be associated with this publication and note the recognition of the family nature of the school embodied in the clan system, which was introduced in 1916 and is still in existence. Lydia Skinner gives perceptive and fair insights into the characters in the making of this history.

James Miller, CBE

Master of the Merchant Company, 1994

INTRODUCTION

When I joined the Mary Erskine's staff in 1964 it appeared to me no more than just another Edinburgh girls' school. I knew nothing of its long history and assumed that it derived its name from some obscure nineteenth-century pioneer in women's education. My first Founders' Day service revealed the depths of my ignorance, and the School's history and traditions soon became as much a part of the background of my teaching life as if I had been reared a Merchant Maiden. The research and writing of this continuation of Margaret Sommerville's History has been a real labour of love and I am privileged to have been given the opportunity to record the history of the School where I spent so many happy years.

The work could never have been completed without the help of many friends and colleagues. I am especially grateful to the Merchant Company, who arranged for the School's early records to be stored in the Library at Ravelston and who gave me access to their own records at Merchants' Hall and the space to work on them; Robin Wilson and Bart Dignan have been unfailingly helpful. Future archivists owe a debt to Dorothy Leurs and Judy Mottram as conservators of the School's records and to La Donna Weber for their cleaning and storage. Numerous former pupils, sadly too many to name, have given me their reminiscences. I hope they will not be offended at remaining anonymous, but to list them would have required a page of telephone directory length. My most sincere thanks go to those colleagues and friends who read through and commented on the text, especially Mary Ambrose, Caroline Batt, Audrey Lawrence, Eileen McCamley, Muriel Jennings, whom I interviewed in Painswick, and Jean Thow; and Patrick Tobin, proofreader emeritus, who shows us in Chapter 10 the vibrant, lively community which is The Mary Erskine School under his leadership. Dorothy Silver has been my constant friendly link with the School while Doreen Waugh has wrestled with the problems of the book's publication.

Considering myself a Merchant Maiden only by adoption, I was delighted to discover during my researches that I could claim to be one of the Family by descent. By chance I discovered that my grandmother and her sister were among the first Queen Street pupils. Their background and future lives reflected those of many of their contemporaries, as I have described in the second chapter of this book. Daughters of a Skye manse, they went on to lives of service in a wider world: one, among Edinburgh's earliest women medical graduates, spending her working life in practice in Madras, the other assisting her doctor husband in Damascus and sending her three sons home to George Watson's for their education. I dedicate this book to the memory of Matilda and Lydia MacPhail and to that of all the Merchant Maidens who have loved and served their School since its foundations.

Note: the following abbreviations occur in the references at chapter ends:

M.C.M.	MERCHANT COMPANY MINUTES
M.M.H.M.	MERCHANT MAIDEN HOSPITAL MINUTES
E.B.M.	EDUCATION BOARD MINUTES
M.M.	'MERCHANT MAIDEN'
D.P.L.	DAVID PRYDE LETTER-BOOK
R.R.L	ROBERT ROBERTSON LETTER-BOOK

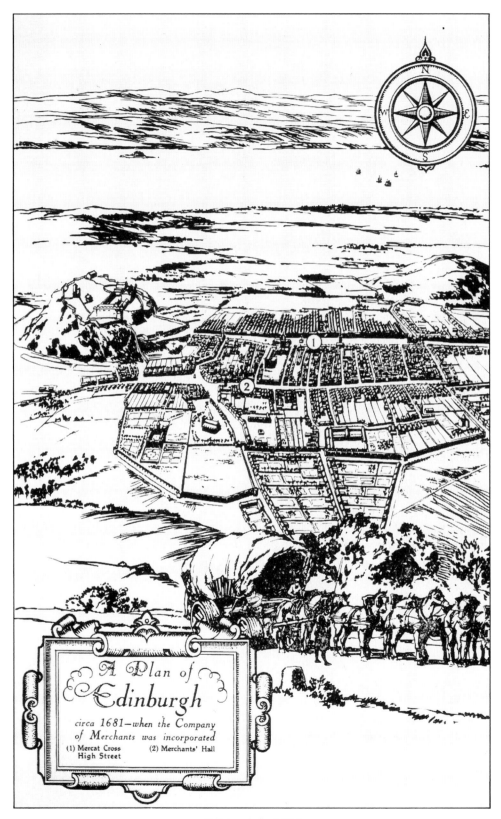

Edinburgh in 1681

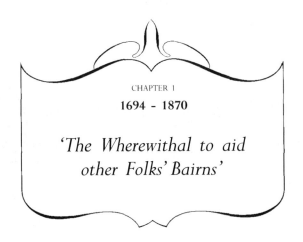

CHAPTER 1

1694 - 1870

*'The Wherewithal to aid
other Folks' Bairns'*

During the summer months Edinburgh's Princes Street is always crowded with visitors as well as with its own residents. They come, naturally, to visit the shops and restaurants, but also to enjoy the dramatic view of the Castle, high on its rock above the spacious lawns and bright flower-beds of Princes Street Gardens. From the Castle the line of the Royal Mile runs down the ridge to Holyrood Palace, and to explore the oldest part of the city the visitor must climb the steep hill called the Mound which connects Edinburgh's Old and New Towns. It has become traditional for Lothian Region to commemorate important local events and anniversaries by marking out, in coloured stones and gravels, a suitable motif, symbol or coat-of-arms on the green lawns adjoining the Mound. In September 1994 the anniversary commemorated was a tercentenary, the founding in 1694 of one of the City's oldest schools. Three hundred years before it was known as the Merchant Maiden Hospital and lay in Edinburgh's Old Town in the shadow of the Castle. Today, renamed after its Founder, The Mary Erskine School has a new home in the green suburb of Ravelston to the west of the city.

In 1694 plans 'for maintaining and educating poor children of the female sex' were first discussed by the Company of Merchants of Edinburgh and a wealthy widow. Born Mary Erskine and now Mrs.Hair, she wished to mortify or to bequeath the sum of 10,000 merks for the maintenance of 'burges children of the female sex' in the city. When Mrs.Hair offered this bequest to the members of the recently-formed Merchant Company and asked them to administer it for her, she was showing her confidence in their integrity as a Company, but she was also imposing a heavy and long-term responsibility upon them. It was, however, a burden which the Merchants seem to have been pleased to accept, and not only because of the implied compliment to their status and integrity. There was a real need in Edinburgh at that time for a charitable foundation of the type that Mrs.Hair envisaged. The 1690s were a period of poverty and depression in Scotland generally and the Merchants were sure that, in view of the obvious need, it would not be difficult to find other benefactors who would be prepared to complement the original benefaction. They estimated that about £20,000 Scots would be needed to endow and maintain the type of institution which they had in mind and so they advertised a 'fund for the lasses', asking for donations which appear to have been quickly forthcoming.

Document dated 1707 bearing the signature of 'Mary Arskine'

It is still uncertain whether the new foundation was finally set up in 1695 or 1696. Certainly it was in the latter year that the Merchants literally opened their doors to the lasses or to 'the Family' as they were to call them, housing the girls in the Merchants' Hall in the Cowgate in

> the Galarie above the Companies hall or Meeting Place with one of the sellars below which has a kitching chimney in it.[1]

The Merchants' Hall in the Cowgate

The new institution was named the Merchant Maiden Hospital, a designation well-known in Scotland where the term 'Hospital' at that period was given to an endowed charitable foundation. Within a few years it had outgrown its accommodation in Merchants' Hall; in any case, it was felt that a move from the Cowgate with its many taverns and boisterous night-life might be advantageous and in 1706 Mrs. Hair gave a further benefaction, purchasing a good house with a garden outside the city wall at Bristo 'towards the use of a hospital to be called the Hospital of Mary Erskine'. In the following year the Merchant Maiden Hospital foundation ensured a place in Scots history, being ratified by the penultimate Act of the Scottish Parliament before its demise on March 25th. This declared

The said Hospital in all times coming to be a free Hospital, with all donations already made but likewise to purchase lands and tenements and others for the use, benefit and advantage of the said Hospital.[2]

In other words, provision was being made for any future development or extension of the purely charitable foundation, the purpose for which the Hospital had been founded.

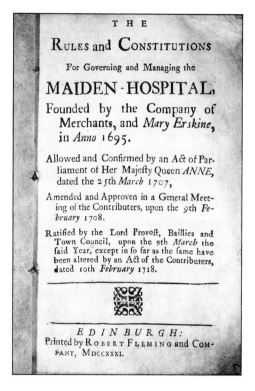

Rules and Constitutions of the Merchant Maiden Hospital.
Rules for Government and Order of the Hospital

Not long after the foundation of the Merchant Maiden Hospital the Company of Merchants was entrusted with another endowment in the shape of George Watson's Hospital for boys, while in the nineteenth century James Gillespie and Daniel Stewart added two more foundations to their educational responsibilities. The finance of these bodies came partly from the original mortifications or bequests but increasingly as time went by from judicious land purchase, investment and loans. The first big land purchase on behalf of their charitable trusts was made by the Merchant Company in 1728 when, due to attainder after the 1715 Rising, the lands of the Keith family came onto the market. The Company purchased the superiority of the town of Peterhead and about 3000 acres of neighbouring land on behalf of the Merchant Maiden Hospital, thus initiating a close

connection between Peterhead and Edinburgh which still continues. Further land pur-
chases were made in the Edinburgh area and in Roxburghshire; the wise management of
these properties would help to support Mary Erskine's original benefaction for generations
of 'the lasses'.

Left *Views of Peterhead* Right *Roderick Gray, Factor of the Peterhead estates*

By the 1860s the number of boys and girls being maintained in the Merchant
Company's Hospitals was almost four hundred and fifty; two hundred of these were day
pupils at James Gillespie's, the remainder boarded at their respective foundations, each
being administered by its own Board of Governors which was responsible for the finances
and for the detailed organisation of its establishment. All the children within the Hospitals
were then loosely designated as 'poor'. Today we would be more likely to call them children in need. They were not necessarily orphans; some had lost one parent, some had
home backgrounds which were in one way or another unsatisfactory, but all were children
whose relatives welcomed the opportunities which the Hospitals offered of free maintenance and the education or training for a self-supporting career.

Merchant Maiden summer and winter dress, 1841

The amount of money held in trust for the Schools was considerable; their first endowments had been swelled by bequests, donations and investment, so that the income available for the children in the three residential foundations was around £12,000. For this annual outlay almost two hundred and fifty foundationers were being maintained at a cost of about £48 each; of this sum about five-sixths was being spent on housing, feeding and clothing but only about one sixth on education. This may by our standards seem a pitiably small sum, but we must bear in mind the infinitely greater purchasing power of money in the 1860s, the comparative cheapness of maintaining a child in institution conditions and the fact that at most levels of Scots society at that period a simple, if not a spartan, way of life was considered normal and acceptable.

The members of the Merchant Company who were particularly responsible for the management of the Hospitals had been aware for some time that changes would have to be made. Social conditions had altered and there was no longer a real need for this type of charitable institution. There was a growing feeling against institutionalised charity and a considerable body of opinion which thought that too small a proportion of the Hospitals' income was being spent on the education of the foundationers. Educationists and writers had long been pointing out the disadvantages of the Hospital boarding system; but it is interesting to see that this violent swing against residential schools for needy children was taking place just at the time when there was a growing tendency among wealthier Scots and English families to send their children to the newly fashionable boarding schools. However, in 1869 after lengthy consideration, the Governors of the Hospitals approached Simon Laurie, a well-known figure in Scottish educational circles, asking him to visit the institutions and to report on the conditions which he found there. As a result of his visits he presented a detailed Report to the Company in July, 1869.

Over a hundred years later this vivid piece of writing can still startle and distress the reader. Laurie was clear-sighted, observant and humane; his empathy with the children in the institutions led him to comments which must have shocked the Hospital Trustees and Visitors. His warm humanity breaks through the words of the official Report:

> The youngest section should have even longer playtime. The little girls should be supplied with ordinary copy-books and pencils. This would much interest the children and give them a pleasant occupation on wet days. The younger division should be allowed to have dolls. Several sets of croquet [should be] allowed besides skipping-ropes and swings. They are over-governessed and over-superintended. I should think it impossible for them ever to move without the consciousness of some eye being upon them.[3]

Laurie's words give us a vivid and often heart-breaking picture of the bleakness of institutional life for children — and we must remember that by the standards of the day the Merchant Hospitals were very well run. The children were adequately fed, housed, clothed and educated, but again and again Laurie stresses the regimentation of their lives.

The Lauriston building 'in the chaste Georgian style' stood in the open ground of the Meadows to the south of the Old Town and had been built for the Merchant Maiden

Pupils at Lauriston

Hospital in 1818. Demolished in the twentieth century to allow for the extension of the Royal Infirmary, it was very similar in style to the present Gallery of Modern Art which was also built as an educational foundation, John Watson's Hospital. Its exterior and public rooms were coldly elegant while the parts of the house not on show were squalidly cramped. Plate-glass windows and chairs carved with the Company's crest were placed in the council chamber where the Trustees met round a table covered with a fine seventeenth-century table-carpet whose border extolled their charitable endeavours; but there were only two baths in the whole building, sufficient to give each girl a bath once a

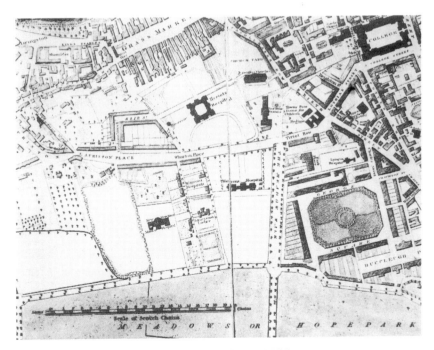

Bristo and Lauriston, 1820

fortnight, and there were only four water-closets, one next to the larder. It is scarcely surprising that a disagreeable smell permeated the ground floor, suspected to be caused by faulty drains.

The Merchant Maiden Hospital, Lauriston

When Laurie visited the Family at Lauriston there were seventy-five Foundationers between the ages of seven and seventeen. They were supervised by an enlightened, warm-hearted Matron, Miss Katharine Bathgate, and three resident Governesses. These ladies

Miss Bathgate

Jane and William Russell, pupils of the Merchant Maiden Hospital and George Watson's Hospital

supervise the girls' conduct, helping to form their personal habits. They also superintend the sewing, the wardrobes and the preparation of lessons.[4]

Nine non-resident teachers were employed, most of them men. These were the only link the girls had with the outer world and with members of the opposite sex unless they were lucky enough to have friends or relatives in Edinburgh to visit. The subjects taught were the basic English, Arithmetic, Writing and Sewing, with Dancing, Music and Singing and French and German for the brighter girls. All classes were chaperoned, a Governess always sitting in the room. Laurie made a detailed report on both teaching and attainment:

[In English] the grammar of the highest class was very weak and excelled by the grammar of boys of eleven at Stewart's. Reading was pleasing. Of literary appreciation [of *Richard II*] there was not a glimmer. Writing of the whole school bold, firm, free and in all respects very good. Herr Weisse's teaching stirs the whole intelligence; he possesses the art of education through instruction in the highest perfection.[5]

Herr Weisse, who was blind, would with M. Schneider and other members of the teaching staff continue to teach the girls after the move from Lauriston.

All the girls were taught sewing and made their own clothes, gingham or wincey dresses, pinafores, flannel jackets, underclothes and nightgowns. They knitted their own stockings and gloves, made sheets and table-cloths and marked all their clothing with their number in cross-stitch. Although some of the older girls were 'allowed to practise machine sewing', most of this work was done by hand. No domestic skills were taught, on the grounds that 'it is not desirable to permit the girls to come into contact with the laundrymaids'. Simon Laurie disapproved of this:

What is good enough for girls out of the Hospital and in a higher sphere of life is quite good enough for girls in the Hospital.[6]

He felt that girls in their final year should have cookery instruction, taking it in turn to cook the School dinner, learning not only basic soup and meat cookery but also 'the best ways of making dishes out of fragments with the help of gravies and sauces'. No doubt the children would have welcomed a taste of such fancy cooking, for their own diet was distinctly meagre and repetitive — daily breakfast porridge, served two hours after rising, the intervening time being occupied with private and public prayer and needlework, a plain unbuttered roll at mid-morning and an evening meal of cocoa and dry bread. Only the midday meal varied between rice or potatoes and milk on Sunday, presumably sandwiched between the day's religious observances, soup with eggs and dry bread or the gastronomic high spot of the week, the Tuesday roast mutton. No butter, fruit, vegetables or sweet foods appear to have been served as part of the regular menu.

The day's pattern was as predictable as the meals. Lessons occupied the girls until mid-afternoon when two hours were allowed for walking and recreation, followed by homework until 8 p.m., although the littlest ones had an hour free for 'play'; in the light of Laurie's suggestions about dolls and games, one wonders what play was possible. Prayer ended the day and the girls retired to the long dormitories where there was privacy neither for pupils nor for the governesses who slept with them. It is not surprising that Simon Laurie was convinced that the lack of family warmth and love, however caring the governesses, was thoroughly bad for children. He appreciated the real interest shown in them by the Governors who saw that they left for careers, mostly in teaching or in dressmaking, who gave them an annual outing to such places as the Falls of Clyde or North Berwick and who permitted Miss Bathgate to

> encourage individuality by permitting each girl to dress her hair as she pleases and to wear round her neck any simple ornament which she may chance to possess.[7]

But Laurie felt that the children's happiness was of a negative kind, their individuality killed by routine and discipline, that the obedience and moral principle in which they had been trained were superficial and that over-protection within school walls bred up children who were totally unfitted to stand up to the stresses of the outside world. He felt too that institution children either thought themselves superior to those whom they encountered when they went out to work or, worse, felt inferior because they had been the recipients of charity. Within the Hospitals the atmosphere was generally oppressive; the resident staff and pupils saw too much of each other and as a result irritations and resentments became exaggerated, leading to nervous tension in both girls and governesses.

The policy which Laurie recommended to the Merchant Company for the Merchant Maiden Hospital was different from that which he advocated for the boys' institutions. He thought that the girls should board at Lauriston until they were ten years old; they should then be boarded out, either with their own families or, if this was not possible (and many foundationers came from other parts of Scotland, some from even further), that they should board with suitable families. Free education and clothing should be given but financial support should only be given to orphans. If this policy were carried out, then the Lauriston building would be available as

> a great Ladies' Day School which would deliver ourselves from the evils of Hospital training, but the present fund would confer a far wider benefit on the Merchant class while opening to the city generally a first-class education for young girls, given under public authority and for a moderate fee.[8]

Even before they had received Laurie's report the Merchant Company were moving towards a solution of the Hospitals' problem. The Master Thomas Boyd, the Old Master and the Convener of the Education Committee had in the last months of 1868 persuaded Moncrieff, the Lord Advocate, to introduce into Parliament the Endowed Institutions (Scotland) Bill which would give the Governors of any endowed institution in Scotland the power to make provision

> for the better government and administration of such government in institutions and

the application of the revenues thereof, whereby the usefulness and efficiency of the said Hospitals and Institutions may be increased.[9]

In plain English this meant that if the Bill became law the Governors of Scottish charitable institutions on the lines of the Company's Hospitals would be able to break the terms of the original benefactions and to allocate the funds, originally available for specific purposes, to other purposes of their own choice.

The members of the Merchant Company seem to have greeted the news of the proposed Bill with enthusiasm when they discussed it in April 1869, but there was initial opposition to its introduction in the Commons, notably from Dr.Lyon Playfair, the Member for the Universities of Edinburgh and St.Andrews, who said

> How unblushing is the reported scheme of reform. The proposal is to degrade respectable citizens by giving them a board for the support of their children in their own homes. It was bad enough when they pauperised them by the Hospital system which nevertheless veiled their shame, but this will be prostitution of a moral duty in a very bare-faced fashion.[10]

'This' was the proposed boarding-out system for the future welfare of the children still living in the Company's Hospitals which was to be the cause of much objection within the months ahead. Playfair's objections, however, had no effect at Westminster and on July 26th, 1869 the Endowed Institutions (Scotland) Bill received the royal assent and became law.

Eight months later in March 1870 a special meeting of the Merchant Company was held to discuss future policy for the residential Hospitals. It was decided that the buildings of the Merchant Maiden Hospital, of George Watson's and of Daniel Stewart's should be converted into

> great day schools for the children of the general community at moderate fees along with the children who were [already] on the various foundations.[11]

Existing foundationers were to be boarded out, remaining day pupils of their original foundations. Scholarships and bursaries were to be established to give further educational assistance to leaving pupils and a Chair in the Science of Commerce was to be established at the University of Edinburgh. The proposals were laid before the Governors of the Hospitals, the Principal of the University of Edinburgh and the Governors of other charitably maintained Edinburgh schools and were received with expressions of warm approval.

All that remained to the Merchant Company and its Education Board was to put them into effect — not in a leisurely manner over a period of years but within five months. In March 1870 the Merchant Company Hospitals were charity schools housing about 250 children; by October the same buildings had been converted into day schools serving about 2500 children and a large staff. The buidings had been rapidly converted to their new use by the architect David McGibbon, teachers appointed, timetables drawn up, additional furniture and equipment purchased and entrance tests held. On September 30th the *Scotsman* printed the report of the Governors of the new Merchant Company Schools from their Chairman, the Master Thomas Boyd. He could assure the public that the rolls of three schools were already closed and his only regret was that their opening could not be marked by some special ceremony, but that shortness of time had made this impossible. The Schools had already opened and were functioning with complete success. To symbolise the new system the names of the Schools would be changed, the boys' Hospitals now to be known as Colleges and the Merchant Maiden Hospital to be renamed the Edinburgh Educational Institute for Young Ladies.

What were the thoughts of the Lauriston Family at this time of change? Margaret Sommerville, the first historian of the Merchant Maiden Hospital, closed her volume by imagining

the last Sabbath evening in the Hospital. The thoughts of the younger girls would be full of the new school to which they would go daily after the holiday. The Matron and the Governesses would meet the leaving girls in the chapel. Miss Bathgate would remind them of the many good things they had enjoyed at Lauriston and give them parting good advice. The Master and the treasurer would visit them; the girls would be told not to think too wistfully of the great new school which only their younger sisters would see, but to remember that they were the last of the many who had known the privileges of an ancient and honoured foundation and that they were expected to uphold its good name as the Merchant Maidens had always done.[12]

Pupils and staff at Lauriston, 1860s

Few relics of the old Hospital have survived, but one evocative photograph remains to us. It shows a group of girls with Company officials or masters and governesses, posed under the portico at Lauriston. The girls, some very young, are wearing light summer dresses of the 1860s. It seems more than likely that the Governors of the Hospital arranged for this to be taken to symbolise the passing of the old way of life for the last Merchant Maidens.

REFERENCES

1   M.C.M., 1694.
2   HERON, PP. 50—51.
3   LAURIE; REPORT IN M.M.H.M., JULY, 1868.
4   IBID.
5   IBID.
6   IBID.
7   IBID.
8   LAURIE; SECOND REPORT IN M.M.H.M., JULY, 1869.
9   M.M.H.M., FEBRUARY, 1870.
10 M.M., 1970.
11 M.M.H.M., JANUARY, 1870.
12 SOMMERVILLE [1], P. 112.

CHAPTER 2

1870 – 1892

'A Great Ladies' Day School'

The Edinburgh Institution for Young Ladies, like the other former Hospitals of the Merchant Company, opened its doors to its new day pupils in September 1870. A few months before it had housed just 75 girls and a small resident staff. Now 1200 girls ranging in age from five to twenty-two years converged on it every morning, not only from Edinburgh, but from the outlying suburbs of Currie, Dalkeith and Musselburgh, crowding the grandly formal stairs and corridors, packed into hastily converted classrooms and dormitories, needing desks and lockers, inkwells and slates, food and cloakroom facilties as well as a full teaching timetable. How was so great a change achieved in so short a time? How could so much sheer administrative detail, planning, frustration and hard work be

Register of the Edinburgh Institution, 1870

fitted into one short summer — and yet achieve what was by all accounts a triumphant success? We can only guess at this, for few details survive of the methods used by the Heads of the Schools in order to ensure that smooth October opening. We can however imagine the sense of exhausted achievement with which they must have faced their assembled pupils at the first Assembly held in each of the new Schools on the opening day of the new session. That moment must have made up for the loss of summer holidays and family life, the hours of poring over applications from hopeful staff and pupils, interviews with parents, class lists, requisition orders, struggles with dilatory tradesmen and the constant backbiting correspondence in the local press, coupled with the openly expressed hopes of many Edinburgh people that the new Merchant Company Schools would never open on time.

The Merchant Company Governors were wise in their choice of Heads for their new Schools and for Lauriston had picked a man of rare quality. David Pryde was thirty-six when he was appointed. Born in Fife of farming stock and educated in the traditional manner at the village school, he had taken his degree at St. Andrews University and at twenty-one had joined the Edinburgh staff of the *Encyclopedia Britannica*. After a period as head of the English department at Glasgow Academy he returned to Edinburgh as a lecturer at the School of Arts, later Heriot Watt College. He was a man of considerable presence, a lively raconteur much in demand as a lecturer and after-dinner speaker, and a popular member of local clubs such as the Monks of St.Giles and the Pen and Pencil Club. A natty dresser, his pupils would see him as a figure larger than life with his highly polished boots and his top hat worn tilted to the side. He had married Barbara Lauder, a member of a notable family of Scots artists, and their home at Fettes Row was cultivated and sociable. Pryde's son, James was himself to become a considerable artist and theatrical designer; his sympathetic portrait of his father hangs today in the School Library.

David Pryde was, however, more than a popular Edinburgh figure with literary and artistic tastes. He was also a considerable administrator, ideally suited to the huge task which faced him in 1870, and a man with a real love of young people and an understanding of their educational needs. Learning, he said, ought to be a pleasant activity and pupils ought to be happy in school. Children naturally enjoyed physical exercise, but mental exercise should be equally pleasant To achieve this teachers should be carefully chosen. He had strong views on the education of women and believed

the degradation of woman has been one of the great calamities of the human race. Had her natural fitness to be the educator of the young of both sexes been long ago recognised as it is now, the world would have been at the present time far happier and brighter.[1]

Believing strongly in equal educational opportunities for girls and boys, his new school offered him every opportunity to put his theories into effect.

On October 18th, 1870 a *Scotsman* reporter visited Lauriston and wrote one of a series of articles on the new Merchant Company Schools. He was obviously impressed by the

David Pryde, portrait by James Pryde

air of smooth organisation and efficiency throughout the building. In a hurried conversion, partition walls had been built across the former great dormitories to provide extra class-rooms, some form of ventilation system had been installed and 'new desks and benches of approved pattern' had been purchased. Cloakroom and lavatory facilities had been installed; we must hope that the former smell of drains had been dealt with. Only the Chapel of the former Hospital remained unchanged, too small for corporate worship and designated now as a lecture hall.

The former chapel at Lauriston

Twelve hundred girls were crowded into the building. Five hundred and sixty eight of them were under twelve. The few over twenty had left other schools some time before but had returned for the sake of the educational opportunities which the Institution offered. Sixty-six of the pupils were original foundationers of the former Merchant Maiden Hospital and were by now either living with relatives, who drew a maintenance grant for their support, or in a boarding-house at Saxe-Coburg Place. All the new pupils had been given entrance tests; three hundred unlucky applicants had been turned down. They came mainly from the Edinburgh area; it was noticeable that only those outlying suburbs served by train could get pupils easily into the city. Leith pupils were being transported daily by special omnibuses. Some parents were so anxious to have their daughters enrolled as pupils that they had arranged for them to be boarded in the city. The reporter analysed the social background of the young ladies and saw them as

> daughters of merchants and well-to-do shop-keepers and members of the professions. Commercial travellers with the shrewdness to be expected of gentlemen of their way of life have been forward to take advantage of the favourable terms presented.[2]

The School was divided into three Departments, Elementary, Junior and Senior, and into about thirty classes, eighteen in the senior School and twelve in the other two Departments. The fees ranged from 12/6 a quarter (65p) for the youngest pupils to £2 a quarter in the Senior School; the pupils were expected to provide 'pencils, slates etc.' The Staff fell into two categories: seventeen full-time visiting Masters, and a large part-time teaching staff with thirty Governesses under Miss Key as Lady Superintendent. The duties of these ladies, some of whom had been on the staff of the former Hospital, were purely supervisory. Each was responsible for the 'appearance and habits' of her own class and for chaperoning her girls, not only during teaching periods but also as they moved about the School between classes, cloakrooms and recreation. The Governesses took their tone from Miss Key. A former Headmistress, her dignified appearance in a rustling black silk dress, jet-encrusted bodice and small lace cap epitomised respectability to parents and visitors, for one of her duties was to act as hostess to the Headmaster.

Miss Key

The Edinburgh Ladies' College

PIANOFORTE INSTRUCTION, without any additional Fee, is given to every Pupil in the Junior and Senior Departments of the College.

Beginners receive two lessons weekly from well-qualified Governesses.

The Governesses teach under the direction of the Music Masters, by whom their Pupils are periodically examined and reported upon.

The more advanced Pupils are taught in classes by the Music Masters and receive a lesson of one hour weekly.

Piano teaching

The one hundred and fifty-seven girls in the Elementary Department learned Reading, Writing, Spelling, Arithmetic and Singing and had, on Simon Laurie's advice, 'object lessons' where they were given items to handle and describe. A grade up, the Juniors had daily lessons in English, Grammar, Geography and History (as was common at that time, the last two subjects were included in 'English') and Arithmetic, French and Writing three times a week, with twice-weekly Music lessons.

The reporter, however, devoted little column space to the younger children and it was obviously the administration of the Senior School that interested him most. Here the day for the six hundred and forty-two pupils began with Prayers in the individual classrooms, followed by fifty-minute classes in English, Arithmetic, Writing and French. Four hundred Seniors took German and there was a weekly piano lesson for every girl in the School, a practice which was not discontinued until 1924. Due to the demands which this made upon the Music staff, eight girls were taught simultaneously, each playing the same exercises; this was such a feature that it was still being illustrated in the School Prospectus in 1895. Only about eighty girls studied Algebra, Geometry and Book-Keeping, while sixty took Latin. About two hundred and forty of the advanced English students had a weekly Literature lecture from the Headmaster, but every girl had one lesson a week in Bible Study and one a day in Needlework, taught by her Governess. After all this, it is comforting to know that there was one period of 'exercise' a week, supervised by a Drill Master, presumably well chaperoned, and the reporter was told that Dancing would soon be added to the timetable.

Catering for such huge numbers was obviously impossible; rolls and milk were available at midday but most girls must have brought their own 'piece', probably eating it in their classrooms. They were allowed into the grounds of Lauriston for supervised exercise, and the reporter was impressed by the opportunity which they had 'to stretch their limbs and expand their lungs after each hour of study', presumably again in their classrooms. He was even more impressed by the Institution's 'change-over' system, designed by David Pryde to ensure orderly and quiet movement about the building. Two by two, led by its Governess, each class moved to its next teaching area once every hour:

> At seven minutes to the hour on the stroke of the bell each class was out in the passage arranging itself. At five minutes the classes began to move; and when the hour struck they were all in their classrooms ready to resume their work and the passages were empty and still. By and by we hit on the plan of playing the harmonium during the change of classes; and it was a pleasant sight to see the long lines of orderly pupils moving along and up and down stairs to the sound of music without any colliding or confusion. The big girls I must confess were inclined at first to grumble about this as being beneath their dignity. But I assembled them together and put the matter to them in this way. 'Unless you keep to the order that I have instituted we shall inevitably fall into inextricable confusion and ruin. Take it as settled that order is absolutely necessary. Besides, when strangers come in, you wish to look your best.' 'Yes!' they cried with one voice.[3]

The anecdote shows us two aspects of David Pryde's character, his handling of his senior pupils and his appreciation of the importance of publicity. On his appointment as Headmaster one of his acquaintances told him that he would never hold down the post:

> 'I would not like to be you — you can't manage twelve hundred girls. It never has been done and never will be done. But make the most out of the Merchant Company for it

won't last long.' Even my own friends became anxious about my personal safety. 'So you are going to try to manage twelve hundred girls. You surely don't know what girls are. They look far more gentle and mum than boys, but they are far more sly, quizzing and mischievous. Man, they'll worry you to death before the year is out.'[4]

David Pryde was well aware of the problems facing him. At thirty-six on his appointment he was not much older than his most senior pupils and a good deal younger than many of his teaching staff:

> I shudder when I remember the anxieties of that time. Here were twelve hundred girls, of all ages from five to twenty, from all the quarters of the land, of different disposition, of different attainments and, like all healthy young people, full of life and fun, ready to notice any idiosyncracy and to comment on it and to giggle over it. Fortunately I was not hampered by any outside interference. The Government had insisted that the head-master, as he had the whole responsibility, should have the appointment and dismissal of the teachers. I was a despot, free to carry out what I thought best.[5]

Fortunate despot! He was the first and only Head who was free of interference from his employers in his management of the school, at least in his early years. Significantly, between 1870—1874, there is scarcely a mention of the Institution in the Minutes of the Merchant Maiden Hospital Governors beyond the regular quarterly statement that 'Mr.Pryde's report was entirely satisfactory'. The sheer scale of their responsibility in their new Schools may have daunted the Merchants and made them glad to delegate responsibility to an obviously competent Head. At the same time, the Company was much occupied with its own business affairs at Peterhead, and the problems of several thousand Edinburgh school pupils may have seemed of minor importance. Given a free rein, Mr.Pryde was able to put his theories of school management into effect, choosing his staff with the greatest care, taking it for granted that there was something good in every child, making the learning process a happy experience and relying on appealing to the better feelings of the pupils rather than disciplining them.

He was fortunate too in the lack of competition from other Edinburgh schools. In the 1870s girls' private education was still in the hands of unqualified but respectable ladies, running small 'Academies' in their own homes and offering little more than a smattering of accomplishments. As a man, backed by a highly qualified male staff and offering an excellent academic syllabus, Pryde could choose his pupils from a wide range of age and ability. He was especially good with his more senior pupils, many of whom were young women of established social position and great strength of character. On one occasion

> when all the complex machinery was in motion and working smoothly and in order and attention seemed to reign everywhere, I was just congratulating myself upon the completion of a worrying task and anticipating a quiet interval to refresh my own mind when the door opened and in filed a long train of young ladies with excitement and indignation upon their faces. They could not get on, they said, with a certain master.

Junior class

David Pryde and pupils

They learned their tasks, they were attentive, they were obedient; but in spite of all they did they could not please him. He was cross, brusque and flustered their nerves so much that very often they did not know what they were saying or doing. 'I sympathise very much with you,' I said, 'but you must consider that we all have faults which require to be looked at charitably by our friends. You should bear in mind that it is his very anxiety for your progress that makes him so gruff.' 'But the other teachers,' they pleaded, 'are so different; they are all so nice. 'Then,' I replied, 'what you complain of will serve a good purpose. The harshness of the one will make you appreciate all the more the niceness of the many. If you cannot look at it in this light there is only one other remedy. Do you wish me to ask this master to resign his situation?' 'No, no!' they cried with one accord. They went away and I heard no more about the matter.[6]

This anecdote reveals a lot about David Pryde — his love of system and order in the complex machine which he controlled, his belief that even a busy Head deserved a little time off and his readiness to discuss a member of his staff with his senior pupils and even in theory to lay on them the onus of deciding the man's future. We can study an 1870s photograph of the senior staff and speculate on the identity of the 'gruff' teacher; surely not Logie Robertson. Head of English and a well known poet in his own right, loved by all his pupils? The popular duo of French nationals, Messieurs Evrard and le Harivel? Herr Schlapp? Robert Robertson, mathematician and David Pryde's successor as Head? Men of character, outstanding teachers, they found at the Institution pupils worthy of them who would fifty years later recall them with love and gratitude. And the portraits of the senior dux pupils of the period are equally intriguing. The young faces look out at us with confidence. They know where they are going when school days end; they are not destined to

Staff at Queen Street

train as milliners and governesses like their recent Lauriston predecessors, but will go on to gain honours in Astronomy and Logic and Mathematics in women's classes at the University, medals at the Edinburgh School of Medicine for Women, entrance Exhibitions at London and Oxford and Cambridge, top places in Civil Service examinations. David Pryde was wise to treat these young women as intelligent adults; they were the seed corn from which the school's reputation would grow.

Early School Dux pupils

Staff appointments could on occasion cause problems. Pryde tells of one applicant for a post who was determined to use every means, fair or foul, to get the situation:

First of all I got letters and visits from his minister, his medical man, his grocer; [next] he had recourse to a plan that was most unscrupulous. If he could not raise himself in my estimation he could at least lower his rivals. He therefore proceeded to assert that they were incompetent, deficient in knowledge, in the power of teaching and in the power of organising. He began to make insinuations about their moral character. One he hinted frequently smelt of liquor, another attended a heterodox minister and a third had an even worse vice. When he had exhausted all his mean and nasty tricks I took a savage pleasure in telling him I could not appoint him.[7]

Prospective janitors also caused difficulty:

I very rashly advertised in the newspapers that I would see candidates on a particular day. At the appointed time the staircase and lobby were filled and the outer door besieged by a motley throng of applicants. They were men of all ages from seventeen to seventy and of all vocations, from that of a teacher down to grave-digger. 'From morn to noon, from noon to dewy eve' I sat interviewing. One man constantly rubbing his knee with his right hand gave me the following account of himself. 'I'm a plooman ye ken and I've had gey hard wark a' my days and I wad like an easy job noo. And I saw your advertisement and says I to my'sel, 'that berth'll sute me, I says.' One elderly candidate when asked about his age said with an elated air, 'I'm just the same age as her gracious Majesty the Queen.' If his royal coeval could govern an Empire why should he not be able to do the duties of a janitor? One correspondent began 'My dear Sir' and ended 'With love to all the family'; another made the admission 'I am a married man but a Christian' and put at the foot of his letter 'P.S. Strick T.T.'[8]

It is pleasant to think of David Pryde pacing the empty, orderly corridors of his building, listening to the hum of busy activity from the classrooms and planning his next glowing quarterly report to his Trustees. He must, in fact, have had very little time in which to relax, for all the Institution's correspondence in the early days fell upon him personally. His handwritten letters from Lauriston to his architect, builders and tradesmen survive:

There is so little room between the seats and the desks that the young ladies cannot get in and out without considerable inconvenience. The Arithmetic masters are complaining of having to speak too loud on account of there being two classes necessarily going on in the Arithmetic Room at the same time. They think that a curtain stretched across the room would in great measure remedy this and at the same time prevent the two classes looking into each other's faces.[9]

Would you kindly send us a box of Brown Windsor Soap at your convenience....you will oblige me by sending to the Institution one box of elastic bands of different sizes and one box of wafers.[10]

And recalcitrant parents got short shrift:

> Sir, I have received your note of Sunday evening and am very angry to find that any person should bring such violent charges against such a very great Institution on such very slender grounds. Your daughter is scarcely a competent judge as since October 17th she has been four times present and eleven times absent and when she has been present she has conducted herself in a very rude manner towards her Governess and Masters. She is therefore a most incompetent judge.[11]

All David Pryde's surviving correspondence is dated 1870, from the early days of the school at Lauriston. It was not until June 1871 that the reopening of the Institution in October was announced, at 'the extensive buildings formerly called "The Hopetoun Rooms" and "The British Hotel"' at the western end of Queen Street. George Watson's College Governors then purchased the Lauriston property, where the school was to remain until its move to Colinton Road in 1932. The Merchant Maiden Governors also purchased a new Boarding House for their foundationers at 10 Bellevue Crescent: the Institution was firmly basing itself in the New Town.

The Edinburgh Institution, Queen Street

By May, 1875 the Merchant Company could feel happy about the state of the Institution. A special Committee which had been set up to report on the Hospitals' finances saw the two boys' Colleges at George Watson's and Daniel Stewart's as still finan-

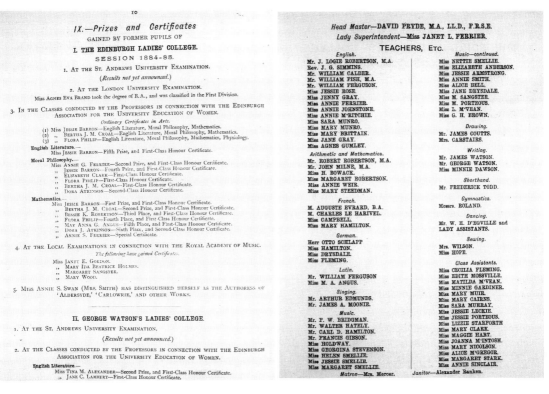

From an early prospectus

cially rather shaky, but the girls' establishment was just breaking even. Fee revenue amounted to just under £8000, running costs of the day school and the boarding house were about £11,000, but rent revenue from the Merchant Maidens' estates covered this and left a small surplus. However, publicity was essential; the public must be kept aware of the excellence of the Company's educational foundations and of the opportunities which they offered, both to fee-paying pupils and to foundationers. Four thousand, five hundred copies of the prospectus of all the Company Schools, including James Gillespie's, were to be printed and distributed; a year later the number produced was 20,000:

> Copies are to go out to Householders of that class formerly comprehended under the designation of 'Ten Pounders' [rate-payers eligible to vote in national and local elections]. 14,000 to be delivered in districts of Edinburgh by Mr.Dowell's 'Weekly List' at a cost of 10d. per 1000 copies; 1000 to be addressed, banded and posted to outlying districts and 4000 to be sent to clergy throughout Scotland.[12]

These early prospectuses have no visual appeal; we are light years away from the large-format colourful productions of schools in the 1990s. Twelve pages of dense type list first the Merchants' Schools' official Examiners:

By the Provisional Orders of Parliament it is directed that 'there shall be once a year an Examination of the Scholars by Examiners appointed for that purpose by the Governors, but otherwise unconnected with the Schools'.[13]

Two University professors, one each from Edinburgh and St. Andrews, and the Rectors of the two Edinburgh Church Training Colleges, held these posts for many years accompanied by 'Miss Gregory, Inspector of Sewing, Edinburgh Board Schools'. Extracts from the Reports of these Examiners of the Institution, George Watson's two Colleges and Daniel Stewart's were printed at length, followed by the names and places of origin of Duxes and Medallists, Foundationers and winners of School Bursaries. Five pages are devoted to University course honours for the boys' schools and to the certificates and class prizes gained by the girls of both the Institution and of George Watson's Ladies' College which had been established on the south side of the city in response to the demand for another large academic girls' school. During David Pryde's years he and his staff had good reason to feel proud of their pupils' successes. As early as 1882 the Institution's seniors, who must have been among the first Juniors at Lauriston, were listed:

At the Matriculation Examination of London University Miss Grace I. Masson and Miss Agnes Eva Brand stood highest among the Lady Candidates and were the only ladies who gained places in the first part of the Honours List. At the St. Andrews University examination Miss Helen G. Brittain and Miss Janet Pithie gained the degree of LL.A.[14]

Grace Masson and her friends

EDINBURGH
MERCHANT COMPANY
SCHOOLS.

THE
EDINBURGH
LADIES'
COLLEGE

HEAD MASTER—ROBERT ROBERTSON, M.A.
LADY SUPERINTENDENT—JANET L. FERRIER.

Session 1895-96.

The College will be re-opened on Tuesday, 1st October 1895.
All information may be obtained on application to the Secretary of the Merchant Company,
14 Hanover Street, Edinburgh.

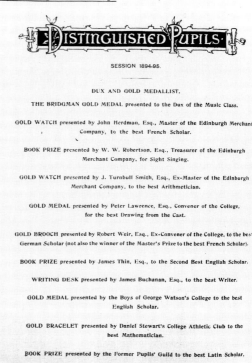

The Edinburgh Ladies' College.

DISTINGUISHED PUPILS·

SESSION 1894-95.

DUX AND GOLD MEDALLIST.

THE BRIDGMAN GOLD MEDAL presented to the Dux of the Music Class.

GOLD WATCH presented by John Herdman, Esq., Master of the Edinburgh Merchant Company, to the best French Scholar.

BOOK PRIZE presented by W. W. Robertson, Esq., Treasurer of the Edinburgh Merchant Company, for Sight Singing.

GOLD WATCH presented by J. Turnbull Smith, Esq., Ex-Master of the Edinburgh Merchant Company, to the best Arithmetician.

GOLD MEDAL presented by Peter Lawrence, Esq., Convener of the College, for the best Drawing from the Cast.

GOLD BROOCH presented by Robert Weir, Esq., Ex-Convener of the College, to the best German Scholar (not also the winner of the Master's Prize to the best French Scholar).

BOOK PRIZE presented by James Thin, Esq., to the Second Best English Scholar.

WRITING DESK presented by James Buchanan, Esq., to the best Writer.

GOLD MEDAL presented by the Boys of George Watson's College to the best English Scholar.

GOLD BRACELET presented by Daniel Stewart's College Athletic Club to the best Mathematician.

BOOK PRIZE presented by the Former Pupils' Guild to the best Latin Scholar.

14

From an early prospectus

Prizes and certificates had been gained in 'the classes conducted by the Professors in connection with the Ladies' Educational Association, the Royal Academy of Music, the Church of Scotland Training College, and the Examinations connected with the Civil Service', while in the Edinburgh University Local Examinations, of ninety-two successful candidates, twenty had gained Honours Certificates and twenty-two prizes, including a two-year Bursary for the best Mathematics paper. Year by year the Schools' prospectus proudly listed its pupils' honours; they were certainly impressive by any standards and were guaranteed to spread the schools' reputation far beyond Scotland. Until 1894 the places of origin of Prize-winners, Foundationers and Bursars were printed in the Prospectus; girls from Edinburgh, Musselburgh, Linlithgow and Lasswade shared honours with others from Inverness, Kenmore, Colinsburgh and Dumfries and from Ceylon, 'Kurrachee', Natal, Bombay, Canada and New Zealand. The Schools were popular with businessmen resident overseas and also with missionaries to whose children the Governors were generous with foundations and awards. The overseas children must have made their own distinct contribution to the Schools, and it is evident from their placing in so many of the prize lists that many of them were able pupils.

By 1891 the Schools' prospectuses were individually printed and produced with an illustrated title-page showing each building. The Governors' names are given, the Company's representatives and those of the Town Council and the Edinburgh and Leith Ministers, followed by a full list of the Staff. Another full list of available Foundations and Bursaries is given; five Foundations by competition for girls of various ages, one four-year Bursary worth £100 in all and forty School Bursaries to cover class fees. Children and grandchildren of present and former Merchant Company members could also claim subsidised places and, as well as these inducements, the Institution maintained a large number of Foundationers under the terms of early benefactions to the Merchant Maiden Hospital. Thirty-seven of these places were in the gift of private patrons who had the right to present a girl of their choice to be educated, boarded and eventually sent out into the world with the gift of a Bible and £9.6.8. The nature of the leaving gift and the names of the patrons reflect the antiquity of some of these benefactions: Roger Hog's, Colonel Blackadder's, Bailie Warrender's and Provost Wightman's Mortifications, the Duchess of Hamilton's Presentation, the Presentation of the Edinburgh Incorporation of Skinners and of the Edinburgh Booksellers' Society, the Magistrates and Town Council of Edinburgh, the Ministers of Edinburgh and Leith.

Patrons were often under considerable pressure from parents who hoped for one of these valuable presentations for the children, and rights of presentation had considerable market value, often being sold off on the death of a patron; it became Company policy to buy out these presentation rights if possible and to transfer the foundation made available into a competitive one. A pupil of the next generation would recall that it was not only possible for a child to pass right through a Company School without a penny of fee being paid but that the paternalism of the Governors was shown in the method of gifting the endowment. Fee remissions were never sent by post; instead on a fixed day, the scholars, bursars and foundationers of all the Company's Schools were summoned to Merchants' Hall and personally handed their cheque or remission slip. The pupils could not only encounter their benefactors in an impressive and dignified setting but could also feel part of the extended family of all the Schools.

In 1870, when the Merchant Maiden Hospital was replaced by the Edinburgh Institute for Young Ladies, a small group of the thirty-one original Foundationers was among the huge intake of day pupils. It was arranged that they should be boarded, first in Saxe-Coburg Place and later in Royal Crescent, under Miss Bathgate, the former Lauriston Head Governess, and a small resident staff. In 1874 the Boarding House moved again, this time to 10 Bellevue Crescent, within easy walking distance of Queen Street.

The Boarding House presented continual problems to the special Company Committee which dealt with its affairs. The house required a great deal of expensive maintenance. Then Miss Bathgate's health broke down and she wished to retire:

> My health is not so strong as formerly which is scarcely to be wondered at after twenty years' arduous service in the Maiden Hospital and forty altogether.[15]

Miss Bathgate's replacement, a widow with daughters who were given foundationer status, was not prepared to be humble and grateful, demanding redecoration for her sitting room,

Miss Bathgate

payment for an evening governess to supervise the girls' homework and holiday mainte-nance for her children.

It was apparent to the Governors that the Boarding House was an expensive luxury; by 1881 the number of its inmates had fallen from twenty-two to sixteen but the cost of running it had gone up to an annual £1588.9.3. The accountants reported that the aver-age cost of maintaining each boarder over five years was £65.8.0. and that under Mrs. Barclay's administration expenses had risen steeply. At the same time the Governors were aware that the examination results of these foundationers were very poor. David Dickson, a member of the Boarding House Committee, wrote in a flurry of underlining:

The source of difficulty has been the exercise of the <u>Patrons' Rights</u>, the <u>presentees of private patrons</u> have been very often of a <u>lower class</u> who from their social position or neglect in early life were unsuitable for receiving such a first-rate education as they get with us. Very often they have been the daughter of the <u>Cook</u> or the <u>Butler</u> or such ser-vants of the patron. All this certainly lowered the value of educational residence in the old Lauriston days and at Bellevue; it would be very desirable if possible to purchase up the rights of patrons. Since Mrs. Barclay became Matron the Home has had a *Mother* over it which it never before had in my time. It presents a serious contrast to my experience of it in 1869 when I was Convener and discovered that the girls were nearly half-starved and got daily doses of Cod Liver Oil as a substitute for Butter![16]

David Pryde reviewed the situation more calmly:

> Five are mostly big girls who have good abilities but are not so earnest in their studies as they ought to be. Six have moderate talent and work very fairly. Four are dull and could not do much under the most favourable circumstances. One is very intelligent and works earnestly and steadily. For this unsatisfactory state of affairs, those who have the charge at Bellevue Cresecent are not to blame — it is the Hospital system. An ordinary Boarding House and a Hospital Boarding House are very different. In an ordinary Boarding House a girl has a great incentive to study hard. She knows that her parents have paid a large sum of money for her board and education and that they expect some visible return for their money — but in a Hospital Boarding House the girls are there through some right of their parents or grandparents or through the presentation of some private patrons who very likely they have never seen — they are little influenced by that great motive, the desire to please. The general result is a greater indifference and a greater want of ambition than are usually seen among schoolgirls. There are several houses kept by thoroughly trustworthy ladies where pupils are boarded at an annual charge ranging from forty to fifty guineas. The Foundationers might be distributed among them. There they would find themselves among intelligent and industrious girls from the country and they could not fail to be struck by such a good example.[17]

This was wise advice and the Committee followed it. The Boarding House closed in the summer of 1881 and the house and contents were sold with the exception of

> furniture to be retained as relics of the old Institution, a Cabinet or Bureau, old Pembroke Table, Wall Mirror and piece of old sewed work. The Pianos, Books and Pictures to be removed to the Ladies' College.

> As regards the other Foundationers at present residing in the Boarding House the Committee instructs the Clerk to intimate to their parents or guardians the usual rates of allowance for outdoor Foundationers, the Clerk to report to the Committee any special cases in which the usual rate of allowance would be considered inadequate.[18]

The Governors had always had a soft spot for the Lauriston Family, and their interest in their Foundationers would continue. Special medical examinations monitored their health, reports on their progress were kept by staff and their school-leaving plans carefully recorded:

She is going into the Telegraph Office ... she is going to learn Typewriting ... as a pupil governess to Dreux, France ... to Godesberg near Bonn, Germany ... to assist in her father's Baker's and Confectioner's shop ... intends being a dressmaker ... going to learn millinery in Glasgow ... returning to school as a Prize pupil.[19]

Some in fact continued their education among the high flyers and did well; but in general these early Foundationers' future plans were a vindication of David Pryde's opinion, echoing that of Simon Laurie in 1869: the Hospital system was not a stimulating environment for children.

One happy demonstration of the Governors' concern for their Foundationers was to continue until 1905. This was the annual summer outing to a beauty spot some distance from Edinburgh. The Governors, their ladies, the Foundationers, the Company Officer and the Janitor would make their way by train and sometimes by steamer to the Falls of Clyde, Dunbar, Peebles or Jedburgh. Lunch and tea would be provided and the arrangements were carefully planned well in advance:

June 9th, 1888. Excursion to Inversnaid. The Secretary was authorised to engage a suitable Violinist to accompany the party. Mr.Robert Blair, proprietor of the Inversnaid Hotel, would charge 7/6 each for Dinner for Governors and their Ladies exclusive of wines. Dinner for Foundationers 3/ each. Dinner for Officer and Janitors 3/ each. Tea for Foundationers, Officer and Janitors 1/ each. Attendance £2.10/ Aerated Waters 2/6 per dozen.[20]

We hope the sun shone: a wet June day at Inversnaid would need more than the violinist and the aerated waters to keep the girls happy while the Governors and their Ladies finished a lunch so lavish that they had no need of the 1/- tea.

An outing in the 1870s

As David Pryde's period of office drew towards its end the School, officially renamed in 1889 the Edinburgh Ladies' College, was in good heart. Numbers remained steady at around the twelve hundred level and the accounts showed a healthy surplus in the mid-1880s. Such profits might be used to fund a small salary rise for teachers, to buy out a right of presentation or be diverted for the use of the Peterhead Estates, which in their turn might help the School Trustees in a period of financial difficulty. The most serious hiccup had occurred in 1878 when the failure of the City of Glasgow Bank had brought ruin to many businesses across Scotland and led to fee arrears and the withdrawal of pupils. The Merchant Company, however, profited by the event, purchasing the Bank's Edinburgh head office in Hanover Street as its new Merchants' Hall. The School's success was based on its reputation for academic excellence, due largely to the quality of the staff it employed. By the year of David Pryde's retirement in 1892 it numbered sixty-six teachers, sixteen class assistants or pupil teachers, a matron and a janitor.

Twenty-three of them were men, all holding senior posts in their departments some of whom had taught in the School since its Lauriston days. Prominent among them were some who were remembered with affection and respect by their former pupils fifty years later. They included Logie Robertson, Head of English, well known in Scots literary circles as Hugh Haliburton the poet:

He alone would have made Queen Street rich as a memory. What he added to its riches in well-nigh two generations we do not attempt to assess. We felt, young as we were, that his literature was life and our daily contact with the pioneer of the Scottish renaissance was an influence that struck deep root in our minds, growing to full consciousness only when we had left him. 'Live' he would say 'and do not spend too long preparing to do it.'[21]

M. Evrard and friends　　　　　　　　　　　　*James Logie Robertson*

The Mathematics Department was a strong one:

> Its teachers were able, its work was of a very high standard and its watchwords accuracy, lucidity and concentrated endeavour dominated the tone of the whole school. A number of our early pupils specialised in Science but there was no specialisation in the school that could eliminate Mathematics and the pupils bred on it seemed to do well in any and every field of knowledge.[22]

David Pryde's successor, Robert Robertson, headed this department until his promotion. Both French and German heads of departments were nationals; the blind Herr Weisse had taught, according to Simon Laurie, 'the only intellectual class in the Hospital' in 1868 and continued to serve the school until 1885 when he retired with an honorarium of one hundred guineas after thirty-one years' service. M. Auguste Evrard joined the staff in the 1870s and remained there until 1905:

> He gave to the school the whole interest of his life. He possessed, along with a highly methodical mind a charm, a human kindness and and a punctilious eagerness to obtain the highest standard of work that were somewhat obscured to the thoughtlessness of youth by the fact that even his mannerisms remained intensely French to the end.[23]

M. Evrard was ably supported by his fellow-countryman Charles le Harivel who was equally loved by generations of his pupils. It is a tribute to their teaching that so many girls went on from Edinburgh for further study in France and Germany or to take up posts as language governesses in those countries or even in Russia. Two future School Headmistresses, Mary Tweedie and Marjorie Chaplyn, went on from the Language department to take University courses and to gain distinctions in them.

The largest department in the School was devoted to Music teaching. Nineteen regular staff and a host of part-time teachers were kept fully stretched with the piano lessons taken by every pupil and with the singing for which the School had a high reputation. At the annual Exhibition and Prize-giving, held at the end of each session in the Music Hall, choral singing under the direction of Mr. Moonie dominated the programme, another feature of which was the famous six-piano performance:

> The choir was trained by Mr.Moonie in the Hall where singing classes were also held, three classes at a time, the good singers at floor level, the hoi polloi up in the gallery. There were about four hundred in the choir and everyone took piano and singing. Mr.Moonie taught classical songs and every year there was a Scottish song on the programme. At the concert each of the four masters had a solo and duet item on the programme, the six best pupils playing the solo and the next six tacked on to play the duet; they practised with their own teachers and then came together for the traditional six-piano item at the Prize-Giving.[24]

These Prize-givings and public performances were important for their publicity value and the Company saw to it that they were reported in detail in the local Press.

Some non-teaching members of the staff also played important roles. Foremost among them were Miss Key, the Lady Superintendent, Mrs.Mercer the Matron, and the Janitor, the latter a less permanent member of the staff until 1892 when, as we shall see, a long-term appointment was made. Miss Key had come from Lauriston and was generally considered to be the power behind the throne at Queen Street:

> Her personality impressed and fascinated the imagination of all the pupils and the younger girls felt a semi-religious awe when they heard the firm steps and heard the rustle of silk that announced her approach.Their memories dwell affectionately on the familiar sight and sound of her bunch of keys and her little work-bag, of the click of her knitting needles and the nimble turns of her crochet hook as she sat and chaper-oned a class in the upper school. Pupils and staff recalled her kindness and sympathy [but] she had a splendid way with culprits; crocodile tears had little effect on her. It was she who said [in 1870] to Dr.Pryde when both were at their wits' end to find time to draw up any time-table, 'Give me the notes and I will bring a workable time-table tomorrow morning' and she and Dr.Pryde's secretary sat up all night and achieved the table which was still the basis of all tables when I finally left Queen Street in 1887. Nothing in the school was too big for her organising capacity and she was as helpful on the social as on the organising side.[25]

Miss Key retired in 1889 and was succeeded by Miss Janet Ferrier, Head of the Elementary Department. With the appointment of a female Head in 1914 the post of Lady Superintendent was replaced by that of Assistant Head.

Mrs.Mercer, the Matron, was the widow of a former Janitor and served under both David Pryde and Robert Robertson, retiring in 1917:

> She guarded the main door, not the one used by pupils; she wore a black bonnet and rang the bell between classes.[26]

Like Miss Key she dressed in deepest black and inspired considerable respect. Both ladies set the tone of the school; Logie Robertson, joining the staff after a period teaching at George Watson's, recalled:

> The first thing that impressed me on entering the girls' school was the perfect orderli-ness and charming quietness of the whole assembly of considerably over twelve hundred girls. It was the manners of a drawing-room at Queen Street.[27]

By the autumnn of 1891 David Pryde's health was failing and he wrote tendering his res-ignation. On hearing of this the Company Preses, Francis Black, wrote from London:

> Time should be taken in filling up the office. I should like someone *outside* and not at present connected with our school.[28]

But the appointment was an internal one and Robert Robertson, Head of the Mathematics Department, who had deputised for Pryde in the past, was offered the post from a short leet of three candidates, one each from George Watson's College and Garnethill School, his salary to be £400 and a capitation fee of 5/- for each non-Foundationer pupil. One condition was set: he must not employ any member of his family on the school staff — a hit at his predecessor who had employed his daughter as school secretary.

David Pryde retired to Chiswick on a generous annual allowance of £500, dying in 1907. The Ladies' College was his lasting memorial:

> My whole existence for twenty-one years was consecrated to this school. I could scarcely do anything without thinking of the Edinburgh Ladies' College. If I devoted my leisure to literature, one of my motives was to restore the elasticity of my mind and make myself fresher and fitter for my duties as head-master. If I lectured and spoke in public it was always with the hope that I would draw more attention to the institution over which I presided. The consciousness of the College enfolded me like an atmosphere and gave its own complexion to everything I said or did.[29]

David Pryde's period as Headmaster had established a great school with a fine reputation. His successor in a quiet way would also win an impressive reputation for himself as well as for the Ladies' College at Queen Street.

Mrs. Mercer

REFERENCES

1–9. DAVID PRYDE, *Pleasant Memories of a Busy Life.*
10, 11. D.P.L.
12. M.M.H.M., 29.6.1876.
13, 14. MERCHANT COMPANY SCHOOLS' PROSPECTUS, 1875.
15. M.M.H.M., 9.8.1877.
16. M.M.H.M., 7.4.1881.
17. M.M.H.M., 3.3.1881.
18. M.M.H.M., 5.7.1881.
19. M.M.H.M., VARIOUS.
20. M.M.H.M., 9.6.1888.
21–23. M.M., 1920.
24. JESSIE LOCHHEAD.
25. M.M., 1920.
26. MARY AMBROSE.
27. M.M., 1920.
28. M.M.H.M., 17.10.1891.
29. DAVID PRYDE, *op. cit.*

Robert Robertson

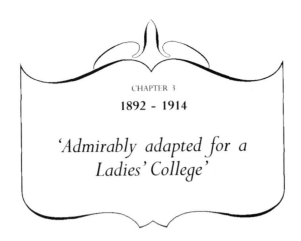

*'Admirably adapted for a
Ladies' College'*

R obert Robertson was a very different man from his predecessor and we know little
about his life away from the Ladies' College. He was an intensely private person and
would never have dreamed of revealing his social life to the world in autobiography. Born
in 1850 at Thornhill, Dumfriesshire, he was educated in the village school, worked as a
pupil teacher and then trained in Edinburgh at the Free Church College before entering
the University to study Mathematics. Graduating in 1874, he spent almost his entire working career at Queen Street. His family life remains a mystery, but we know that he lost a
son in the War in 1916, the year of his own death:

> Less impressive perhaps to a superficial observer he possessed a quiet, impelling strength
> of character, a sure love of justice, a power of long endeavour that produced steady and
> eager work and deep if silent respect. His laughter was all the heartier for being heard
> less often and his quiet, almost shy appreciation of real fun was a delight to witness. He
> gave in no light sense his life to his work, subordinating all outside interests to his great
> goal — the good of his school.

> Few schools can boast of a Head to whom its thousands of pupils have presented each
> one a personality and a life history and still fewer of one in whom the individual inter-
> est in his thousands of old girls lasted as long as any one of them came to claim it at
> their old school.[1]

This tribute is confirmed from his surviving correspondence in a Letter Book of 1894—
1912. He wrote daily one or more letters on School business to the Merchant Company
Secretary, Alexander Heron. These letters, often of two or three pages, in longhand until
1909, must have taken up much of his day; there are also others appointing new staff,
dealing with kindness and concern with the problems of existing staff members, worrying
about the supply of gas for the bunsen burners and the poor quality of boiler fuel, discussing necessary building repairs with the architect and drawing up elaborate graphs
showing how pupils travelled to school. Above all his concern was with his pupils, from

the high-flyers recommended for posts to the delinquents who disrupted the School's smooth routine and who might tarnish its reputation:

> I thoroughly approve of the pupils having relaxation from their mental work and at the beginning of every session I strongly recommend the senior classes to take it daily in the form of walking whenever weather permits. But that is quite a different thing from attending an evening Dancing Class from 5.15 to nearly eight o'clock and which necessitates exposure to the evening air. I cannot help thinking that Miss Louise's lessons had the first claim upon her attention last Thursday evening after the neuralgia had settled.[2]

> After a full discussion in which your years of faithful and efficient service were frankly acknowledged and sincere regret expressed as regards the serious illness through which you passed last year, the Governors could not help coming to the opinion that your illness had left permanent effects seriously affecting your efficiency, especially for conducting classes in a large school. It is with the deepest regret that I find myself obliged to discharge the present painful duty. Our intercourse during the past six years has been uniformly pleasant and I trust we shall part as friends.[3]

> I understand that you are a trustee of .... who has been a pupil here since May 1902. I think it my duty therefore to inform you that a letter has just come into my hands which she admits to have been written by her to a former class fellow, the contents of which are of such a nature that I cannot allow her name to remain longer on our rolls.

Five days later, having suggested a meeting with this gentleman:

> Your telegram reached me at my home address shortly after ten o'clock on Saturday. I set out at once for school and found that the Janitor had left before your arrival. From school I went to the Merchant Company offices in Hanover Street in the hope that I might find you there. I regret having missed you but I did not anticipate a call from you on a Saturday.[4]

> During her school course here which extended over seven years Miss Mary Tweedie gave ample evidence of decided natural talent and a capacity for sustained, well-directed and intelligent application. All her school work was performed with the greatest faithfulness and her examination papers were marked by orderly, logical arrangement, thorough mastery of details, originality and felicity of expression.[5]

> The Dancing Staff visit Atholl Crescent [the Elementary Department] for the first and second periods every Tuesday and Wednesday and it is necessary that they should be at Queen Street not later than 10.55. After one period's work they go to George Square for afternoon teaching. They find the work of these days very exhausting owing to the frequent moving from place to place. If they walk between Atholl Crescent and Queen Street their boots have to be changed twice. It can easily be understood that the difficulty and delay is increased on wet mornings. I beg to recommend that in the

A dancing class

circumstances the ladies should have the use of a cab. The total expenditure for 76 hires would be between £2 and £3 per annum. Were this arranged it would be unnecessary for the teachers to change their boots and they would be fresher for their work.[6]

Robert Robertson was particularly aware of the strain to which his pupils were subjected through the demands of their school courses, through pressure from ambitious parents and through preparations for the regular public performances put on by the Schools at Prize-givings and Concerts:

After the fullest preparation by the teachers of the Elementary and Junior departments it is necessary to have two or three combined rehearsals [in School] where at least four hundred pupils are crowded for from an hour to an hour and a half on a hot July day. There follow in close succession the Rehearsal and Exhibition in the Music Hall. Last year

a] On Saturday the pupils were present in the Music Hall from nine o'clock till after two o'clock.

b] On Monday they were again present from ten o'clock till after two.

c] On Tuesday they were seated in the Orchestra from half-past two to half-past five.

When it is remembered that healthy Senior pupils find the ordinary routine work of the School as much as they can face towards the end of the session it will at once be evident that such a severe strain as the foregoing involves cannot but be prejudicial to the health of the little ones. I was informed by the father of one of our pupils that after the Closing Exhibition his little girl completely collapsed and that during the whole of August she remained in a state of extreme nervous prostration. One hears more frequently than one would wish the cry that no work is done in the Merchant Company Schools during the last month of the session. While everything is done to keep the regular work of the school going during the closing week it is quite manifest that it cannot receive full attention while so much time and strength is demanded for rehearsals. There exists a pretty strong feeling in the minds of a considerable number of the parents that the performance is too elaborate and savours too much of the stage.[7]

Robert Robertson's clash with his employers, the Merchant Company, highlights the problems faced by the Schools' Heads in the 1890s. They no longer had the freedom to operate their own small empires with the minimum of Company interference, which had been the case in the early days. Then the Schools had run at capacity with long waiting lists and finance had not been a problem; the Ladies' College had a healthy annual surplus and knew that its investment funds would be available to finance any extraordinary outlay. But things were changing fast in Scottish education. The Endowed Institutions Acts of 1878 and 1882 had done for other Scottish foundations what the Act of 1869 had done for the Merchant Schools; across Scotland many former hospitals in their turn became secondary schools for the children of the middle class while new foundations were also

Merchants' Hall, Hanover Street

established. In the field of girls' education these included St.Leonard's at St.Andrews, three schools in the Glasgow area, and, more seriously, St.George's, Edinburgh, founded in 1888 and, on the South Side, St.Margaret's, founded in 1890. Middle-class parents of daughters now had day or boarding options and were not forced to send their children to board in Edinburgh in order to attend the Merchant Company foundations. The Education Act of 1892 brought more problems for the Governors of fee-paying schools with the extension of free grant-aided secondary education throughout Scotland and the establishment of local Secondary Education Committees; in Edinburgh one member of the Merchant Company was represented along with a member of the Heriot's Trust. The new secondary schools could offer scholarships as well as free places and were tempting to parents who might find it hard to finance their children's education at a fee-paying foundation.

Robert Robertson and senior pupils

Along with these changes came a new funding system for Scottish schools. In 1897 the system of Science and Art Grants which had been administered from England was transferred to Scotland and became widely available for secondary and technical education in 1898. Schools with recognised Science and Art Departments could now count on an annual grant administered by what was still called the Scotch Education Department, whose inspectors would report on their worthiness to receive government support. If the Merchant Company schools were to qualify for grant status, they would have to make sure that they came up to the exacting standards set by the Department.

The system of examination was also changing. The Ladies' College girls regularly sat the Edinburgh University Local Examinations which had been first introduced in 1865. By 1883 there were seven hundred and forty-six female candidates in the Edinburgh area; it was useful as a system for testing clever girls and their only means of securing entry to University courses. In 1888 the introduction of the Scottish Leaving Certificate gave the Universities a benchmark by which candidates could be assessed for entry, and in 1892 the University Preliminary Examination, open to boys and girls, meant that the University

Class Group

Edinburgh Ladies' College.

SESSION 18 97 . 98

Miss Davina McDonald   Class X

CLASS MARKS

	English	Hist. & Geog.	Arith.	Latin	French	German			Music	Times Absent	Times Late	Pro-gress.	Con-duct.	Signature of Parent or Guardian.
FIRST QUARTER,	85	70	99	84	84	82			G	0	0	S	V.G	D. McDonald
	84	61	84	83	80	85								
SECOND QUARTER,	83	73	94	91	89	88			G	0	0	V.G	V.G	D. McDonald
	82	68	83	75	76	84								
THIRD QUARTER,	86	68	95	94	96	87			V.G	0	0	H.	V.G	D. McDonald
	84	64	80	82	80	81								
FOURTH QUARTER,	84	83	99	96	96	90			V.G	0	0	V.S	V.G	
	82	70	85	83	81	83								

EXAMINATION MARKS.

	English	Hist. & Geog.	Arith.	Algebra	Geom.	Latin	French	German	Remarks.	Signature of Parent or Guardian.
First Examination,	48	85	86			86	93	88	Satisfactory	D. McDonald
	83	69	80			74	81	86		
Second Examination,	88	82	98			96	95	82	Satisfactory	D. McDonald
	76	74	93			83	76	80		

EXPLANATION OF MARKS.

MUSIC.   V.G.=Very Good; G.=Good; M.G.=Moderately Good; F.=Fair; Def.=Deficient.
PROGRESS.   H.S.=Highly Satisfactory; V.S.=Very Satisfactory; S.=Satisfactory; F.=Fair; Un.=Unsatisfactory.
CONDUCT.   V.G.=Very Good; G.=Good; F.=Fair; Un.=Unsatisfactory.
The number placed under *Arithmetic, Latin, French,* and *German,* indicates the Division in which the Pupil is classified for these subjects.
For comparison the percentage gained by the Pupil is entered in the upper division of each square, and the average percentage gained by the Class in the lower division.

N.B.—This Card to be kept clean, regularly signed and returned.

J. REID, 78 QUEEN ST., EDINBURGH.

Mark Sheet

Locals were no longer necessary; already the Ladies' College girls had been taking the national Leaving Certificate for three years.

Enrolments at the Company Schools began to fall off in the early 1890s. In October 1893 Robert Robertson made a special report to the Education Committee on the situation. Nine hundred and fifty-seven pupils had enrolled, compared with eleven hundred and thirty-five in the previous session; this shortfall represented a loss in fees of about £1000. Over the previous four sessions there had been a 28% decline in applications, the greatest loss in the Edinburgh area, south-east Scotland and the area north of the Forth. Normally he would expect one in every eight of his pupils to come from Leith; now there were only six enrolments. He had no doubt that the reason for the decline in numbers (matched in the other Company Schools) was the opening of the new Higher Class or secondary schools in Leith and the Edinburgh suburbs as well as in provincial towns like Linlithgow, Callander and Stonehaven. Parents would naturally prefer to send their children to the local school, saving fees, travelling expenses and boarding costs. At the same time many parents were moving out into the Edinburgh suburbs and liked the convenience and economy of having their children walk to school and come home for the midday meal. A period of financial recession generally was not helping the situation, as many children who might have stayed on either left early or were transferred to cheaper local schools to take their qualifying examinations.

The Company must fight to get its pupils back. Advertising its successes was essential; the Schools' examination results were outstanding, yet they were not being published. A link must be established with the Royal Academy of Music and pupils should begin to take its examinations; results here should also be made known to the public through the Press. Lunchroom facilities at Queen Street were lacking and were urgently required; the Board must consider rebuilding at the back of the building to provide accommodation:

> We must rely on doing everything in our power to promote greater efficiency and to convince parents that by sending their children to the Ladies' College they get a better ultimate return than by sending them to schools where fees are low or where secondary education is free.[8]

The Governors considered this Report at a meeting where it was announced that the College's surplus for the year was £46.17.0., while building costs for alterations amounted to over eight hundred pounds. The situation was serious. Two thousand pounds would have to be borrowed from Daniel Stewart's funds in order to cover the teachers' salaries at Queen Street. The Convener said:

> Of the influences adverse to this School, some are of a temporary character but others are likely to be permanent and may be expected sooner or later to affect all the Company's Schools. These demand the very serious consideration of the Governors, yet never was the School more efficient and never was the tone of character of the School better than at present.[9]

He regretted that the Leaving Certificate results could not be published, since 84% of Leaving Certificate candidates had been successful, while in French and German the percentage of passes had been 95% and 97%; in all subjects except Latin the pass rate had been between 30% and 50% above the national average.

The Governors did not hesitate, and things moved fast. Exactly a year later the Convener reported:

> Considerable uneasiness was felt at the beginning of last session by reason of the falling-off in numbers. It was resolved [1] to bring the outstanding educational advantages of the Institution more prominently before the public. [2] to extend and improve the recreatory and refectory accommodation at the College. The former has given effect to the issue of an artistically illustrated prospectus followed by a highly successful entertainment on the part of the Elementary and Junior pupils which filled the Music Hall to over-flowing; the additions to the School buildings are still in progress. Although it is too early to estimate the full effects of these measures, the results so far are most promising. If we look at the figures for the opening of the new session the enrolments amounting to 1156 may seem insignificant but when placed against a decrease of 133 last year I am justified in characterising the result as satisfactory.[10]

The 'highly successful entertainment which filled the Music Hall to overflowing' was the event which Robert Robertson had criticised for the strain which it had placed on his pupils. The Company had ensured its Press coverage; from now on all Spring and Summer Exhibitions would be brought before the public as essential publicity material.

Internal changes had already been introduced on Robert Robertson's appointment with a new timetabling system where pupils remained as far as possible with the same subject teacher for several sessions. It is typical of the Head's caring attitude that he thought the school day was too long and that it should end at 3 p.m. except for practical subjects. A Library was badly needed and on Logie Robertson's initiative the Board was persuaded to advance £30 for books and bookcases; it was pointed out that Queen Street was lagging behind here, as George Watson's Ladies' College already had library facilities; both Schools would charge an annual subscription of one shilling to borrowers. The two Ladies' Colleges also began discussions on Science teaching; this resulted in 1895 in the introduction of Physiology and Zoology classes for Seniors and Botany for Juniors. A year before lectures on Health by a lady doctor had been introduced, again for the Seniors. In 1892 a teacher of Shorthand was appointed for the Civil Service examination candidates; 1895 saw Typewriting and Practical Cookery along with Book-Keeping and Scientific Cutting-Out and Dressmaking. The Head and the Board saw the importance of providing two types of course, an academic one leading to certification and probable University entrance and a practical one for the less academic pupils. This proved very successful and excellent results were achieved in Civil Service Examinations [first place in Britain in 1895 and second in 1896], and in entrance to the Edinburgh School of Cookery for which leaving Bursaries were available.

5

FEES FOR THE ENTIRE COURSE.

		Per Quarter.
1. ELEMENTARY DEPARTMENT,	.	£0 12 6
2. JUNIOR DEPARTMENT—*Lower Division*,	.	1 7 6
Do. —*Upper Division*,	.	2 0 0
3. SENIOR DEPARTMENT,	.	2 10 0
Do. —*Advanced*, .	.	3 0 0

Pupils who have passed through the Senior Advanced Classes may take separate Branches at the Fee of One Pound per Quarter for Music; 10s. per Quarter for each of the other Subjects.

The Fees are payable quarterly in advance. The Session extends from the beginning of October to the end of July, and the Quarter days are :—1st October, 17th December, 1st March, 15th May.

Written notice of the withdrawal of Pupils during the course of the Session should be sent to the Head Master *not less than fourteen days previous to the end of a Quarter*; otherwise, liability will be incurred for the fee for the next Quarter.

Parents are requested to co-operate with the Headmaster in carrying out the following regulations :—

1. Pupils must be punctual and regular in their attendance, orderly in their habits, and polite in their conduct both in and out of School.
2. When a pupil is absent, intimation of the reason should be sent at once to the Head Master. No excuse, except illness, is regarded as satisfactory for absence or neglect of lessons.
3. No Pupil is allowed to leave during school hours without a written request signed by the parent or guardian and addressed to the Head Master.
4. School-books, &c., should be marked with the Name and Class of the Pupil, so that any article found may be at once returned to the owner.
5. Pupils who have suffered from any infectious disease, or who have been living in a house where such a disease has occurred, must not attend School until they bring a Medical Certificate stating that all danger of infection is past.

N.B.—As soon as the Summer Holidays begin, building operations will be commenced with the view of providing a new Luncheon Room and a spacious Recreation Hall on the most approved principles. It is expected that both rooms will be ready for use soon after the beginning of next session.

4

THE EDINBURGH LADIES' COLLEGE,
QUEEN STREET.

The Pupils will re-assemble after the Holidays, on *Monday, 1st October 1894,* in the extensive Buildings Nos. 70, 72, and 73 Queen Street (West End), and adjoining Hall.

The Institution provides Young Ladies with an Education of the Highest Class, qualifying them for taking advantage of a University Course.

The Course of Study embraces all the Branches usually taught in the principal Institutions and Boarding-Schools for Young Ladies, and includes English, French, German, Latin, Arithmetic, Mathematics, Science, Writing, Book-keeping, Shorthand, Drawing, Pianoforte-Music, Singing, Drill, Dancing and Calisthenics, Needlework, Cookery, and Sick-Nursing. Courses of Lectures are given during the Session on Subjects likely to interest and instruct the Pupils.

Religious Instruction is given in all the Classes.

A Gymnasium has been added to the College, and all the Pupils have the opportunity of receiving instruction in Gymnastic Exercises.

There are Three Departments,—Elementary, Junior, and Senior.

The Pupils are carefully arranged in Classes, and these are subdivided, where necessary, for various subjects of study. The number of Pupils in each Class is limited, and promotion from one Class to another depends upon progress as tested by periodical Examinations, the results of which are sent home for the information of the parents.

The Pupils in the Senior Classes are presented for the various grades of Leaving Certificate granted by the Scottish Education Department. These Certificates are now accepted as an equivalent for most of the Professional Entrance Examinations.

There is a Luncheon-Room in connection with the College, and hot luncheon is supplied during the winter months at a moderate charge.

The Class-rooms are kept scrupulously clean, and careful attention is given to heating and ventilation. The whole School-Buildings are annually inspected and reported on by Sanitary Authorities.

An addition has been made to the Premises, whereby larger and better-lighted rooms have been obtained for the Elementary and Junior Departments.

Tennis Courts have been provided for the use of the Pupils.

From a prospectus of the 1890s

Physical Education was another field which had been neglected in the School's early days. Drill classes were provided under a Drill Master though it was perhaps timely that he was dismissed in 1893 for 'coming to school in a condition unfitting him for his duties'. He was replaced, in line with current physical education theory, by Margit Lund from Sweden who taught gymnastics and Swedish Drill; a year later she was joined by Miss Henriksen and both women were given full-time appointments. Outdoor sport facilities had always been a problem because of the School's situation, although an arrangement with Daniel Stewart's College had allowed tennis to be played on their courts in the evenings since 1883. But the Head and the Board were acutely aware that the College had no facilities at all for exercise during the school day; David Pryde before his retirement had continually pressed for recreation facilities, pointing out that he was forced to send the younger children up to Princes Street Gardens for supervised play.

In 1889 the Merchant Company had purchased for £30,000 the estate of Falconhall at Morningside. There was a good classical mansion with extensive grounds, and the Board were of the opinion that it was

admirably adapted for a Ladies' College. Had the time not come when extra schools should be commenced in different parts of the city in place of incurring large expenditure by enlarging the present School buildings?[11]

A gymnastic class

Both of the George Watson's Colleges were interested in the site, but matters hung fire until the summer of 1892 when the Master, Treasurer, Convener and Heads of the four schools paid a visit to Blair Lodge School, Polmont, 'in connection with the buildings and appliances at the Merchant Company School'. A boarding school for boys, Blair was extremely progressive, offering

> a Commercial Room where each boy had a japanned tin box for his books, had his money deposited in the School bank and his banking done for him by the Commercial pupils. Music rooms with walls deadened by sawdust, well-fitted Chemistry and Physical laboratories, workshop and forge, centrally-heated study rooms for each pair of boys and an Art Room with a rack containing two hundred drawing boards.[12]

The deputation was obviously excited by Blair Lodge, and for a time the Board seriously considered establishing a boarding school for either boys or girls at Falconhall. Probably the recession in the early 1890s brought a change of mind, coupled with an adverse report from the architect David McGibbon on the suitability of the house as a school and the expense of converting it.

The grounds, however, provided exactly what the two Ladies' Colleges needed in the way of sports facilities, and in the spring of 1893 a groundsman was appointed, tennis courts laid out and a pavilion built. Until the playing fields at Inverleith were opened in 1923 Falconhall remained the centre of the school's sporting life and generations of girls travelled on the Morning-side Station tram to play hockey or tennis and, for a time, golf on the site where the Dominion Cinema now stands. The 1895 prospectus shows the first photograph of a rather bleak field; backed by a charming little pavilion, eight girls in heavy dark clothes and wearing hats are preparing to play two sets of doubles while a groundsman is improbably cutting a stretch of coarse grass with a very small hand mower. By 1899 the photograph chosen to illustrate the prospectus is much livelier: the same grounds-

Tennis team

Hockey team

The Edinburgh Ladies' College

Juniors

man is posed with the same mower, the tennis courts are still occupied but a group of girls, still in hats, is engaging in some ladylike stick practice. In 1906 this photograph, distinctly dated, is still in use but the prospectus is enlivened by a hockey team group wearing comfortable gym slips; the only hat in sight is being worn by the coach.

From 1895 the Prospectus developed a new image and was obviously an important feature for selling the school. Printed on glossy paper, as well as the traditional lists of Staff, bursars and prizewinners and information about the organisation and curriculum in the three different departments, there are eight photographs of some quality, all obviously carefully posed. These include a view of the School facade and the one of the Falconhall field mentioned above. There are also interior groups. Several pinafored little girls and their teacher stand reading in a classroom decorated with ferns in china pots and a Pears Soap calendar; 'Tuesday' is written in elegant copper-plate on the blackboard. 'Sewing

Juniors

Class' is posed in the main school Hall. It is 1.25 and at least fifty girls with lap-bags round their waists are sitting in tiered rows, supervised by three teachers; the same potted palms appear to have been shifted from the Elementary department to enliven the scene. A group of Juniors dancing to piano accompaniment is superimposed on another view of the Hall, while the famous eight-piano teaching system is also illustrated. A large group is shown in 'The new Recreation Hall' and the back page shows two views of Peterhead, stressing the traditional connection between the town and the Ladies' College.

The most interesting of these photographs is the one of the Recreation Hall. It shows a large group, some apparently preparing for country dancing while others sit on the benches round the wall. Gaslights hang from the beams below skylights; the floor is parquet, the dado pitch-pine. Any former pupil of the pre-Ravelston era will instantly identify with the scene and can people 'the Rec.' with herself and her own friends, for it remained unchanged until the demolition of the old building and was almost the only part of the School where girls from different classes and age-groups could mingle socially.

From the start the Queen Street building had given problems. Part of it was a large terraced house which had been used as a hotel, part had been designed as a suite of entertainment rooms, used for concerts and dances. The School Hall was famous in Edinburgh as having been the setting for a recital by Chopin on his Scottish tour. Elliptical in shape, with a glass cupola supported by Greek caryatid figures and with a raised area which could be closed off by sliding doors, it provided not only a formal setting for concerts and social evenings but was also used for classes in Singing, Sewing and (most improbably) Cookery. The Schools' architect, David McGibbon, could do nothing radical to convert the building to make it suitable for school use, due to lack of funds and to the fact that no major alterations could be carried out except during the summer holidays. The general policy was one of minor repairs and redecoration as needed. Continual efforts were also made to purchase adjoining properties with a view to extending the School to east and west but these were generally unsuccessful. It was the falling rolls of the 1890s which led to the first project, the building of the Luncheon Room and the Refectory. It was agreed in 1894 to make a two-storey extension at the rear, connected to the main building by a gangway. This would be partly financed by an improvement grant from the Burgh Committee. The work, which would cost over £4000, involved removing the roofs of the Sewing and Singing rooms but would provide a teachers' Common Room over the common stair in no. 73. In January 1895 the new rooms were formally opened by Lord Woolner, tea and cakes being purveyed for the occasion for £15 by the school caterer.

The new Recreation and Luncheon Rooms

The new Luncheon facilities were advertised in the Prospectus:

The Governors have recently erected a spacious and well-equipped Luncheon Room which affords ample facilities for every Pupil partaking comfortably of a substantial luncheon. Bread, Milk, Coffee, Cocoa, Soup, Meat and Potatoes are supplied to the Pupils at a moderate charge.[13]

By 1906 this had been extended to read 'and in summer Pudding with Stewed Fruits'.

The scheme, however, had its teething troubles. In the first week fifty-five dinners and one hundred and thirty-seven soups had been sold but by the third week these numbers had almost halved. The food, apparently cooked elsewhere and sent in to be reheated, was almost uneatable:

Soups had been sent smoked, badly flavoured, insufficiently cooked and too cold while bread was burned, sodden and badly soiled.[14]

The purveyor promised to mend his ways but the catering remained unsatisfactory until the Edinburgh Café Company got the concession in 1899, 'giving the greatest satisfaction to all parties'.

Further progress came in 1899 when the Board considered the installation of electric lighting. Ignorant and rather fearful of such advanced modern technology, they decided to go to the top for advice, 'the Professor of Electrical Engineering at the Heriot Watt College being empowered to report'. The report obviously being favourable, the lighting was partially installed, although many of the classrooms would retain their gas-lighting well into the twentieth century along with the coal fires which were their only method of heating. But the building was structurally unsound in parts as well as generally inconvenient. Alarmed by a fall of plaster in 1903 'which narrowly missed a pupil', the Board began to consider a major scheme of reconstruction at the east end of the building. This would involve total demolition and would consequently pose appalling accommodation problems, so appalling that the whole scheme was at risk of being shelved altogether. One possible way of solving the problem of housing pupils during the demolition period was to use James Gillespie's Hospital building at Bruntsfield. This small and poorly-endowed foundation was being phased out (it was eventually handed over to the Edinburgh School Board in 1908), and for some time there was serious discussion by the Company and by the Scottish Education Department on building a new school on that site. By 1908, with the sale of Gillespie's imminent, the Department was firm: something drastic must be done to the Queen Street building or the grant would be withheld.

In the summer of 1908 the architect Washington Browne was appointed to draw up plans to demolish and rebuild the whole front and the centre section of the building on the understanding that the number of pupils accommodated would not exceed eight hundred. The Scottish Education Department intervened, setting the number at six hundred and insisting that Elementary departments should be established on both the north and south sides of the city. Lists of suitable properties were drawn up and in 1909, No. 16

Atholl Crescent was purchased for £2950 and adapted for use at a cost of £1020. The younger pupils, in what came to be called the Preparatory department, were established for the new session of 1909 under the charge of the Misses Munro and their staff. The rebuilding on the Queen Street site was shelved and the architect paid off; no more than a general repainting and refurbishing took place in the old school, but Robert Robertson was delighted with the new arrangements:

> The most notable circumstance has been the removal of the Elementary Department to new premises at 16 Atholl Crescent which has added greatly to the comfort and effi-ciency with which the work at Queen Street has been carried on. Additional space has been gained, a more logical and systematic arrangement of the classrooms has been ren-dered possible, congestion in the corridors has been relieved, class movements during school intervals greatly simplified and stair climbing much reduced. The Examination Hall into which the old Elementary classroom has been converted has proved service-able in many ways. At Atholl Crescent the suite of rooms is very complete, containing gallery accommodation for senior and junior classes, well-furnished class-rooms, music room, rooms for gymnastics, dancing and play, luncheon room, staff rooms, store rooms and museum. They are well lighted, bright, sunny, fresh, airy and well-furnished. The open-air verandah behind has been of great benefit but the playing space in the centre of the garden has been of very little service, as the gravelled surface has proved abso-lutely unsuitable. So much was expected from the open-air playground where the drill exercises might have been given. The slope behind has been very tastefully laid out by the janitor who personally supplied nearly all the plants.[15]

The Education Committee, when it paid its state visit of inspection, was very much impressed, especially by

> the laudable attempts by the Misses Munro and their assistants to make the rooms attractive by the introduction of works of art on the walls.[16]

The Preparatory department would feature largely in the School's publicity material until it was returned to Queen Street in 1921.

Fortunate Juniors, enjoying space and light, the verandah and the Garden (which was eventually concreted as being kinder than gravel to small knees). Their older sisters were still in the inconvenient dark rooms at Queen Street where even a quick lick of paint, a new hot water system and the installation of a telephone were not likely to keep the Education Department quiet for long. By January 1912 the question of using the Gillespie's building as a temporary overflow was on the cards again and again rejected on grounds of cost. Instead a deal was struck with the owners of 69 Queen Street, the Royal Scottish Nursing Home. The Company purchased a house at 19 Drumsheugh Gardens for them and the College was able to expand sideways; with extra space available the demolition scheme was at least feasible, and in the summer of 1912 Hippolyte Blanc was appointed as architect. His scheme of reconstruction included not only extensive class-

Juniors at Atholl Crescent

room and service facilities but a play area at the rear and a roof garden. The estimated cost of the new building was just under £46,000; the Building Committee was horrified but sanctioned the plans and demolition began, much to the irritation of the College's neighbours, Messrs. Tods, Murray and Jamieson who complained bitterly about the dust. Inevitably the work proceeded too slowly; in May 1913 the Education Board was alarmed to learn that St.George's School was erecting a new building for a mere £25,000 and

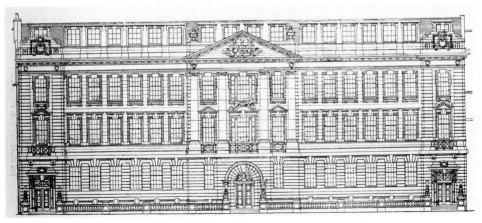

The proposed new building

Class 7 Junior

Mr. Blanc was taken firmly to task. As the East Wing rose slowly, so did its cost and the Company became increasingly alarmed. When Robert Robertson announced his retirement in 1914 the structure was still incomplete and was not to be ready for occupation until 1915 when a new Head had taken his place. The second phase of reconstruction to the west, planned by Blanc in his original scheme, was shelved on grounds of cost and patriotism and was never achieved.

Life at both Queen Street and Atholl Crescent was vividly remembered by those who were taught there before 1914. Mary Crawford travelled to Atholl Crescent by train from Gogar, catching the train at 7.40 a.m. after a twenty-five minute walk to the station. There was no official uniform; all the little girls wore white pinafores, taken home to be washed on Fridays, and white gloves for dancing lessons. They entered Atholl Crescent by the steps to the basement which housed the cloakrooms, the lunchroom and the verandah where they played on wet days. On the first floor a long room with tiered seats ran the width of the building; Miss Sarah Munro taught at one end and Miss Russell Rodger at the other. On the top floor was another large room for dancing, drill and play.

Barbara Smith remembered that each child on arrival at school had to knock at the door of the Miss Munros: 'Wee Miss Munro and Big Miss Munro'. On entering they were greeted by name and asked 'and how are you today?', to which they replied with a curtsey 'Quite well thank you Miss Munro.' If it was your birthday you were allowed to wear a gold paper crown all day as a Princess and to choose another girl as your Prince; she wore 'a glengarry with peacock feathers.'

Mary Crawford also recalled their busy timetable by the time they attained 7 Junior,

THE EDINBURGH LADIES' COLLEGE

Is distant from (*a*) Princes Street Station about 5 minutes' walk ; (*b*) Waverley Station, about 12 minutes ; (*c*) Haymarket Station, about 15 minutes.

TRAIN TIME-TABLE.

(1) Trains arriving at *Princes Street Station* at 8.22 and 8.52
A.M.

Leave	Leith	...	...	at 8.1 and 8.31
	Newhaven	...	...	8.3 ,, 8.33
	Granton Road		...	8.6 ,, 8.36
	Craigleith	...	...	8.12 ,, 8.42
	Murrayfield	...	...	8.15 ,, 8.45
	Dalry Road	...	...	8.19 ,, 8.49

Return trains at 3.3 and 3.33 p.m.

(3) Trains due at *Waverley Station* at 8.24, 8.48 and 8.58 A.M.

Leave	Longniddry	...	...	at 7.52 and 8.38
	Prestonpans	...	...	8.0
	Inveresk	...	...	8.7
	Joppa	...	...	8.34
	Portobello	...	...	8.37

Return train at 4.0 p.m. ; to Portobello and Joppa at 3.0 p.m.

(5) Train due at *Haymarket Station* at 8.32 & 8.40 A.M.

Leaves	Kirkliston	...	...	at 7.54
	Ratho	...	...	8.31
	Gogar	...	...	8.37
	Saughton	...	...	8.42

Return train at 3.5 ; to Kirkliston at 3.24 p.m.

(2) Trains due at *Princes Street Station* at 8.25 and 8.55 ; from Mid-Calder at 8.45 A.M.
A.M.

Leave	Mid-Calder	...	...	...	8.22	
	Balerno		7.53 and 8.23			
	Currie	...	7.59 ,, 8.29			*Via Main Line.*
	Juniper Green		8.5 ,, 8.35			
	Colinton		8.10 ,, 8.40			
	Slateford	...	8.17 ,, 8.47			
	Merchiston	...	8.21 ,, 8.51	8.41		

Return train at 2.30 and 3.30 p.m. ; to Mid-Calder at 2.15, 4.2 and 4.25 p.m.

(4) Train due at *Haymarket Station* at 8.31 A.M.

Leaves	Dunfermline	...	...	...	at 7.49
	Inverkeithing	...	...	...	8.1
	North Queensferry	...	...	8.8
	Dalmeny	...	...	...	8.14
	Turnhouse	...	...	...	8.21
	Corstorphine	...	...	...	8.30

Return train at 3.54 p.m. to North Queensferry and Inverkeithing : to Dalmeny and Dunfermline at 4.19 p.m. ; to Turnhouse, 4.34 p.m., and to Corstorphine, 3.14 p.m.

(6) Train due at *Haymarket Station* at 8.49 A.M.

Leaves	Bathgate	...	...	...	at 8.5
	Uphall	...	...	...	8.19
	Drumshoreland	...	...	8.24
	Ratho	...	...	...	8.31

Return train at 4.19 p.m.

(7) Train due at *Princes Street Station* at 8.48 a.m., *leaves* Barnton (for Cramond Brig) at 8.30, and Davidson's Mains at 8.34 a.m. *Return* trains at 3.7 and 4.7 p.m.

CAR TIME-TABLE.

Times of departure of morning Cars which leave in time for School :—

		A.M.	A.M.				A.M.	A.M.
Bernard Street, Leith ...	...	8.18	8.28	Morningside Drive	...	...	8.25	8.29
Colinton Road	...	8.15	8.25	Murrayfield	...	...	8.30	8.35
Comely Bank (Cable) ...	...	8.28	8.32	Newhaven	...	...	8.10	8.20
Gorgie	...	...	8.30	8.35	Portobello and Joppa ..	...	7.50	8.5
Golden Acre (Cable) ...	...	8.15	8.20	Nether Liberton	...	...	8.10	8.14
Jock's Lodge	...	8.15	8.30	Seafield, Leith	...	...	8.5	8.20
Morningside (Church Hill)	...	8.30	8.34					

NOTE.—The Tramway Company issue Tickets at 1d. each to scholars if purchased in bundles of sixty. These Tickets are available at any time of day, any day of the week, all the year round.

23

Travel arrangements

'James'

which included 'meanings', grammar, Bible, copy-book writing and sewing. In the summer their work was exhibited, including under-garments 'threaded with ribbons of each class's colour.' On Friday afternoon there was a sing-song for the whole school and the best piano players performed their pieces. Once a year, two by two in a long crocodile, they made their way to 'the big school' for medical examination where the School Doctor might report

> Five hundred and sixty-five cases of measles, four hundred and fifty-six of whooping cough, forty-one of diphtheria and four of typhoid with two hundred and fifty-four afflictions of the throat, mainly tonsils.[17]

Jessie Thom (Mrs.Lochhead) entered Queen Street in 1902 and left as Dux in 1914. She travelled by horse-tram from Leith to Pilrig, changing there onto a cable car to Waverley and then often walking the length of Princes Street. The older girls wore 'any type of dress, even an old party dress at times; we tried to start a uniform with a navy skirt, a white blouse and a blue and red striped tie in my senior year, but it was not taken up. For Gym if you were posh you wore bloomers, otherwise an ordinary frock, a summer dress for tennis and a gym-costume for hockey. You wore boots to school and changed them for slippers; everyone needed at least three pairs of shoes. They were carried along with books in school bags; they were never worn on the back, that was for boys. Queen Street girls either slung them over one shoulder or carried them'.[18]

Changing clothes and boots took place in the basement cloakrooms, known to generations of Queen Street girls as the Dungeons. Marjorie Chaplyn remembered them as 'dusty and dank with, at the end, a forbidden, cobwebbed, eerie space; I was dumbfounded to learn that when the school moved in from Lauriston that twilit region must have been the recreation room'. She was of the generation before the move to Atholl Crescent and remembered the littler ones being sent for 'a little walk' to stretch their legs, 'tiptoeing upstairs from their class-room, along the corridor and down the other stairs, two by two'.

Before 1914 all the classrooms were lit by gas and heated with open coal fires. The Janitor came round the classes with a taper on a long pole to light the gas jets; the junior classrooms had no gas lighting and classes were sent home early on dark evenings. The Janitor also made up the fires; the fortunate girls were the ones at the front of the class, the ones at the back might shiver, though caring teachers operated a rota system and on really cold days brought everyone round the fire. The Janitor's other task which brought him into contact with the girls was 'to enter in lateness on your report card when you arrived at school'.

The Janitor from 1892 until 1928 was James Auchinachie, loved and respected by generations of old Queen Street pupils. An Aberdonian and former regular soldier, he had fought at Tel-el-Kebir and taken part in the expedition to relieve Khartoum:

> At Queen Street he played the part of the perfect Janitor, half tyrant, half parent. A man of many parts, a true friend of school activities. He has acted in our plays, raised our curtains, taken our photographs, gone our errands and bullied our dilatoriness. Our

Janitor is of the pioneer stuff that peoples colonies, ready to set hand to anything and never too busy to help a friend.[19]

James provided spare red and blue elastic chest expanders for girls who had forgotten to bring their own to dancing classes which took place in the Hall; the best dancers did a demonstration eightsome reel at the Senior Social for the top forms when party dresses and gloves were worn and everyone had a tiny dance programme with a pencil attached. The girls danced with each other and with the Staff, and after refreshments a play was performed. The Hall was in constant use. 'Granny' Wilson and 'Aunty' Hope took sewing classes there, Mr.Moonie rehearsed his choir and cookery was demonstrated to the Seniors from a gas cooker. The girls sat in rows in the tiered area and took notes on the recipe; the instructions always ended with the same words, 'serve on a dish paper garnished with parsley'. Jessie Thom recalled 'there was a great row one time when the girls handed in their note-books for a cake recipe, ending it with these words'. Teacher baiting was mild enough — an alarm clock in a cupboard for Miss 'Bunny' Angus ('there was always capering in her class') and a mouse pinned to Dr.McIntosh's coat-tails — but teachers were popular and were recalled years later with affection: Miss Graham calling her dancing class 'naughty naughty darlings', Mr.Moonie 'irascible, unpredictable, temperamental' who was so likely to fly off the handle that a chaperone had to sit in his classes, Mr.Cormack 'with his lazy voice and whimsical smile who refused to be hustled'. Marjorie Chaplyn recalled:

Handwriting

Many staff were former pupils; all loved the school and handed on the torch of its tradition as a few of their ilk have done throughout the centuries and will always do.[20]

1913 saw the retirement of one of the giants on the staff, Logie Robertson, who had taught English in the school for over thirty years. The next year saw the Head's retirement. In poor health, the war imminent and with continual problems and delays over the rebuilding scheme, he felt that it was time to hand over to a younger person and to enjoy a retirement which would be sadly brief. The Education Board felt that the time had come to appoint a female Head as George Watson's Ladies' College had already done; she should not be over forty, should hold a British honours degree and would receive a salary 'not more than £550'. There were twenty-nine applicants for the post, four of them former pupils, including Mary Tweedie; all were aged between twenty-nine and thirty-nine. The Board's choice fell on Mary Clarke and she became headmistress in the autumn of 1914, just after the outbreak of the war.

Coronation pageant, 1911

REFERENCES

1. M.M. 1920.
2-7 R.R.L.
8, 9 M.M.H.M. October, 1893.
10 M.M.H.M. October, 1894.
11 M.M.H.M. March, 1889.
12 M.M.H.M. June, 1892.
13 Prospectus, 1896.
14 M.M.H.M. January, 1895.
15 Principal's Report, 1909—1910.
16 M.M.H.M. October, 1909.
17 M.M.H.M. July, 1892.
18 Jessie Thom (Lochhead).
19 M.M. 1920.
20 Marjorie Chaplyn.

Mary Clarke

CHAPTER 4

1914- 1924

'Be active and not passive learners'

Mary Clarke was thirty-three when she became Headmistress of the Edinburgh Ladies' College. An Aberdonian, daughter of a University lecturer in Education and a mother with roots in Peterhead, her home background was academic, lively and stimulating. She went up to Girton in 1900:

> Because I was the eldest of six and my father's salary was small I had to practise the strictest economy. But I worked hard and played tennis hard [and] found myself Captain of the Cambridge Women's Lawn Tennis Team and achieved a First Class in my Tripos, my subjects English and German.[1]

After two years' postgraduate work she trained as a teacher and taught at Roedean and St.Leonard's where

> I was at last finding my feet as a teacher and becoming a person in my own right. Imparting knowledge had never been a difficulty; but I had been very slow to acquire the personal authority on which all good teaching depends and which comes hard to those who are diffident by nature. One morning Miss Bentinck-Smith sent for me and, showing me an advertisement in 'The Scotsman' for a Headmistress for one of the Merchant Company of Edinburgh's two large day-schools for girls, commanded (I can use no other word) me to apply for the post. I was genuinely taken aback, indeed horrified. But my pleas of youth, shortness of experience and personal unfitness were brushed aside so, docile to the end as an underling, I made my application and to my surprise was appointed as headmistress of the Edinburgh Ladies' College.[2]

'Diffident'; 'docile': these are not words which anyone who remembers her could apply to Mary Clarke, yet the official photograph taken for her appointment shows a very young and rather uncertain woman. She wrote later:

> I entered on preparations for taking up my new post with some trepidation. I had to

address myself with all my might to the task before me which was the management of a school of over seven hundred girls with an age range of from four to nineteen years, under wartime conditions.[3]

To these girls, accustomed to an Olympian headmaster figure, this slight young woman was a revelation:

> She brought with her a new outlook on education which came to its full fruition after my time, but to us then she brought a refreshing and exhilarating stimulus. At first all were rendered almost speechless as she swept into a classroom, descended swiftly upon us, posed a rapid question to which she expected an equally rapid answer. She was here, there and everywhere it seemed, galvanising us into activity of which we had not dreamed ourselves capable. We soon grew to enjoy the exhilaration of her approach, her expectation that we should be active and not passive learners, that we should use our initiative and be self-reliant in all things.[4]

Mary Ambrose as a child of ten recalls the new Head calling the whole School together to introduce herself to them on her arrival at Queen Street and the fact that she soon knew every girl by name.

Mary Clarke, fresh from the stimulating atmosphere of St.Leonard's, found the Ladies' College old-fashioned and male dominated:

> All academic departments except Modern Languages were in the hands of men teachers, many of them men of great personal and academic distinction. To preserve the proprieties former pupils of a suitable age were retained at a pittance to act as chaperones. The staff numbered over seventy, almost all older than I was, artificially swollen by the so-called 'governesses' and the large number of music teachers of both sexes.[5]

She had to gain the trust of the Merchant Company Education Board and the support of the Former Pupils' Guild who, like the staff, were suspicious of her youth. She also had to tread warily in Edinburgh's social life; in Aberdeen her family had an assured position, but in Edinburgh women teachers, even headmistresses, sat well below the salt. There was much to be changed but she had to move carefully. In her early years she acknowledged considerable social and professional help from Dr.Charlotte Ainslie, Headmistress of George Watson's Ladies' College. The war, although it was to bring considerable problems, also helped her to achieve her aims. Men and women on the staff left for war work; women teachers could be promoted to posts of responsibility while the older men who remained on the staff became valued colleagues, although

> I had my difficulties, which arose if any kind of criticism or reproof was called for, for it was undoubtedly a delicate matter for a young woman to criticise without offence a man much older than herself. [I learned] to delegate as much responsibility as possible to the staff; the wisdom on occasion of turning a blind eye to what was happening or

had already occurred; and the folly of working systematically beyond one's physical strength.

In a patriarchal country like Scotland it was natural enough that an aura of unconscious superiority should surround the Men's staff-room. Not to have had a staff-room reserved for male teachers would have been unthinkable. But the specialists with honours degrees as such decidedly held themselves aloof from ordinary graduates and non-graduates. The head of a department taught the A or brightest forms, the deputy-head taught the B or next best forms while everyone else available taught the C and D average and sub-average forms. I suppose any one of the specialists would have agreed with me in principle that more skilled teaching is needed for intellectually weak than for able pupils, but the rigidity of the arrangement was bound up with considerations of professional prestige which made it almost impossible to alter.[6]

The system proved so unalterable that it was in use in some departments in Queen Street in the 1960s.

Mary Clarke with a Domestic Science class

Changes in school administration were tactfully introduced; almost all have stood the test of time. With a passionate belief in the importance of history and tradition for any organisation, Mary Clarke was behind the institution of Founders' Day.

The prefects

The new wing

The class numbering system (VI for the top classes and I for the lower ones in the Senior School) is still with us. So is the Prefect system which she introduced as early as 1916, the Clan system, Morning Assembly, Girl Guides, the School Song, the Guild Room, Clerical and Commercial courses, Gym and Dancing displays, Swimming, school Sports, school Societies, drama productions of quality, Parents' Meetings, Staff meetings and school uniform. Years ahead of her time, the unmarried Head even introduced evening sex education lectures by a woman doctor for senior pupils, though these were at parents' discretion. In ten years as Headmistress Mary Clarke gave the College its lasting reputation as a progressive girls' school.

The new building was almost ready; inevitably, however, not when promised. It was not until the summer of 1915 that the east wing could be occupied and almost immediately the inevitable complaints began. The building was cracking, warping, leaking, noisy through lack of soundproofing. It was, however, custom-built as a school and a considerable improvement on the west end and on the nineteenth-century dining and recreation extension. The cost of the new building was estimated at over £23,000; the Board, stretched financially through more work at George Watson's Ladies' College, decided to call a halt here and no further building was carried out.

Fundraising postcard

The War dominated the lives of everyone in the school for Mary Clarke's first four years. A month before its outbreak the Scottish Education Department was sufficiently out of touch to write asking whether the Head would like to employ a native German language assistant for the next session; a year later some parents were writing asking to withdraw their daughters from German classes taught by Herr Hinkelbein who had been many years on the staff, and who continued to teach throughout the war, although there was a significant drop in the numbers of girls taking the subject. Various members of staff went voluntarily into war service, men through Territorial call-up and women to serve as VADs. The Headmistress's Annual Report in 1915 showed that the School had responded with enthusiasm to the call to help the war effort. Six hundred and fifty 'knitted comforts' had been sent to the Forces, fifty-five dozen eggs had been collected 'for the wounded' and the profits of the 'Merchant Maiden' magazine were being invested in War Loan. One Junior form had hung Lord Kitchener's portrait in the classroom, draped with the Union Jack, and a poignant entry in the school magazine described the marriage and widowing of a former pupil within two months, the young husband being killed at the front in August.

A year later the impact of war was much greater. 'Air-raids' had taken place over Edinburgh in April, leading to much absence, and 'many girls and staff were suffering from over-strain and debility'. An austerity note had been introduced in serving school lunches: those who chose to eat meat had to surrender food coupons, but a meatless dish was always available as well. Knitted comforts continued to be turned out in vast quantities, many by the former pupils who had transformed their pre-war German Circle into a work-party. The School had established a strong link with a Red Cross hospital at Rouen where three beds named after Mary Erskine had been endowed. Sphagnum moss collection and cleaning was a popular activity, toys were collected for Forces families and Serbian children, and hundreds of postcards were collect-

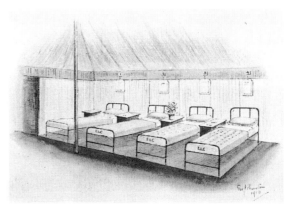

The Mary Erskine ward at the Rouen Hospital.

ed at Atholl Crescent and made into a scrap screen for a local hospital. Miss Tweedie did her bit for the war effort by delivering a lecture on 'German methods of assimilating annexed territory in Schleswig-Holstein, Alsace-Lorraine and Poland', while former pupils were reported serving as nurses at the front and supervising munition workers. Some women staff were serving in the WAAC.

Economies were made to help the war effort. Prospectuses were not being posted but must be collected; the allowance for school medals and prizes was being halved while the Dux gold watches (cost £30) were to be replaced by silver models at a cost of £8.15.0. By 1918 a mountain of knitted comforts must have been produced and were being sent to Mesopotamia as well as to France, demonstrations on Food Economy were being given to girls and parents by the Domestic Science pupils and a War Savings Association was raising about £35 weekly. Over two hundredweight of soap had been collected (presumably for recycling) and girls went to help with the berry-picking at Auchterarder. The summer of 1918 brought the Spanish 'flu epidemic with the compulsory closing of all the city's schools and the cancellation of closing concerts and prize-givings, a source of deep resentment in Dux pupils who missed their moment of glory.

The War years were recalled fifty years later by a Senior Prefect who saw herself and her contemporaries as

a naïve generation who did not know that the eye of innocence was slowly closing over Europe. We loved Rupert Brooke and were moved to tears that Julian Grenfell's naked earth should be so very warm with spring. We knitted shapeless balaclavas and ill-paired khaki socks. We hunted for sphagnum moss and collected War savings stamps. The brilliant ones clutched parchments with 'Prize Resigned' after all but one subject. We knew our King and Country if not Kitchener needed us .... and the latter had needed many of our male staff. We feared for our fathers and brothers with the immature anguish of adolescence.[7]

When peace came in 1918 girls, parents, former pupils and staff could look back proudly on their record of war service. In June 1919 the Company's schools got a holiday when the Peace Treaty was signed and a month later there was a memorial service for the fallen of the schools at St.Giles' where even the Ladies' Colleges remembered losses. In the autumn life returned to normal. Masters who had been in the Forces returned, the War Fund with a grand total of £1100 was wound up, the U.F. Moderator took a Peace Thanksgiving service and the Juniors produced a Peace Pageant. The first Usher Hall prize-giving was symbolic of new beginnings. At the end of the ceremony large quantities of flowers, fruit and eggs were collected and distributed, not to the troops but to 'the needy and sick' of the city, a gesture with which the school's founder would have been totally in sympathy. For many years the Queen Street Prizegiving was marked by the prizewinners laying flowers on the table as they received their prizes; these were delivered after the ceremony to the City's hospitals.

The post-war years brought problems for many of Scotland's independent schools. Rising costs and falling incomes hit parents and school managers alike and some old foundations found it impossible to survive on their original endowments. Of the thirty-four independent schools recognised under the 1882 Educational Endowments Act, only thirteen were left by the 1920s. Some like Merchiston and Glasgow Academy had survived

The first Guide Company

by setting up trusts and becoming private companies, but many went under, most passing into the hands of the Local Education Authority. The Merchant Schools, however, were fortunate in their endowment and administration. In 1895 the Company had amalgamated all its educational trusts under a central committee with a common fund to be used as required by any of its foundations. This provided a large investment income which could finance building and improvement as and when it was needed. The Scottish Education Department's requirements from 1900 for Science and Art provision led to these funds being used in the pre-War years to provide laboratory and Art Room facilities at all the Company's schools.

Another result of the amalgamation of funds was the establishment in 1895 of a Superannuation Scheme for all teachers in the Company's schools, started with a £7500 grant from the Endowments Board and said to be the first scheme of its kind in Britain. James Gillespie's, the least viable of the Company schools, was transferred to the local authority in 1908 as a fee-paying Higher Grade School. The following year the Company's educational Trusts were amalgamated under 'The Merchant Company Endowments Order', again simplifying financial administration and releasing funds as needed. With this sound backing and with the support of the S.E.D. grants, the Company's schools could face the post-war years, confident in their reputation and in a growing demand for admissions. In 1919 the Ladies' College roll was eight hundred and seventy girls.

It has been said that the first question asked of any newcomer to Edinburgh between the wars was 'Where do you live?' and the second was 'Where are your children at school?' The answers to these questions, and especially to the second one, immediately placed the new resident socially into one of three bands. Top in the pecking order came the private single-sex boys' and girls' schools, most of them offering boarding as well as day facilities. Next came the Merchant Company day schools, all still single-sex and providing schooling for about three and a half thousand of Edinburgh's children. The remaining schools fell into two categories, Higher Grade endowed foundations such as George Heriot's charging fees and local authority schools providing free education. The Company's schools were deservedly popular with Edinburgh parents. Their academic reputation was high, their facilities for sport and extra-curricular facilities far ahead of what the local authority could provide. Smart uniforms, a high standard of discipline and above all low fees made them popular with Edinburgh parents and there was fierce competition to get children in, preferably at the beginning of Primary, for once 'in' the child's educational future with the Merchant Company imprimatur was assured. Children and grandchildren of Company members were assured of places and usually of financial support; other fortunate entrants might also apply for financial help as foundationers with fees covered and grants towards books and clothing. Thus, in spite of economic depression, the Company schools continued to flourish.

Mary Clarke's school years at the end of the century had been spent at Aberdeen's High School for Girls. She recalled the inadequacies of the system:

Science was only a name. The class repaired once a week for one period to a demonstration room where we watched the master set up experiments in physics which

A Science class

O . [?]   Session

I. EDINBURGH LADIES' COLLEGE.

1. EDNA MARY ANDERSON, 4 Magdala Crescent.

Age—7

Father—Thomas Anderson, schoolmaster, was a teacher in Donaldson's Hospital in 1913. After the war, Principal of the Presbyterian College of St. John's, Newfoundland. Dead. Was not a member of the Merchant Company.

Mother—Alive.

Total income of family is derived from boarders, and fluctuates.

School attended—Bruntsfield School, 2 sessions; Edinburgh Ladies' College, session 1925-26.

Past benefits to applicant—Restricted fee of £1 per term for one session.

Brothers or sisters—

  Names and ages—William Alexander, 5.

Circumstances rendering application necessary—Owing to the father's death, the family has been left without the means for an education such as they would have had. The Earl of Home has considered the case for presentation to the Foundation, which becomes vacant in 1927.

Principal's report—Attendance, regular; progress, very good; conduct, very good. Fee for next session, £4, 11s. per term.

2. MARY ISABEL ARMOUR, 74 Comely Bank Avenue.

Age—11.

Father—Archibald James Armour, clerk, with City Corporation. Resided in Edinburgh for 60 years. Dead. Was not a member of the Merchant Company.

Mother—Alive.

Total income of family—About £30.

School attended—Edinburgh Ladies' College, 5 sessions.

Past benefits to applicant—Restricted fee of £1 per term for 3 sessions.

Brothers or sisters—

  (a) *Names and ages*—Alfred James, 14.

  (b) *Names of such of them as have attended Merchant Company Schools*—Alfred James, Daniel Stewart's College, 3 sessions.

  (c) *Modification of fees or other benefits received there*— 1 session. Restricted fee of £1 per term.

Circumstances rendering application necessary—Death of father.

Principal's report—Attendance, regular; progress, fairly good; conduct, very good. Fee for next session, £5, 5s. per term.

Applications for Foundations

invariably failed. It would have made no difference to the pupils if they had succeeded, as no coherent explanation of them was ever given. Of biological science or teaching
on sex there was of course nothing. Physical training was a matter of marching and
exercises done to music. Art consisted mainly of freehand drawing of plaster casts of
flowers. The greatest wants in our social life by modern standards were the lack of any
training of the emotions, the lack of corporate school activities and the entire absence
of scientific training. There were no school societies, no prefect system, no opportunities for the development of social responsibility and leadership. Schools existed for the
training of the mind and that was a full-time affair. Other considerations were not
pressing.[8]

She found the Ladies' College a mirror image of Aberdeen High School in 1914 and set
out with determination to show the Company and the girls that there was life outside the
classroom. High on her list of priorities was 'a need to stimulate common loyalties and
enthusiasms'. The school, as the oldest of the Company's foundations, had a long and honoured history which must be preserved for future generations. Two years after the War
ended she had the opportunity to exploit this history with the fiftieth anniversary of its
foundation. With the other Company schools a series of commemorative events, sports,
concerts and receptions took place while a special Jubilee issue of the 'Merchant Maiden',
lavishly illustrated and edited by Mary Tweedie, recalled the past fifty years in a series of
articles as well as outlining the history of the original benefactions and of the Merchant
Maiden Hospital. Even the tinies in the Elementary Department were reminded of their
antecedents:

> Little women at Atholl Crescent, listen to what I am
> going to tell you, and when you have heard be
> grateful and happy. When your grandmothers came
> to school at the Edinburgh Ladies' College fifty
> years ago they came to Queen Street and were
> taught in the room that you occupied when the pipe
> at Atholl Crescent burst. Do you remember? It is a
> big room and may once have been pretty but the
> windows look north. That means that the sun would
> never look in all day — think of your sunny class-
> rooms! They learned to write, those quaint little
> grandmothers; they certainly did not paint and cut
> out Man Friday with a blue jacket and red trousers.
> Hush! How shocking![9]

Two years later, to commemorate the anniversary of
the move from Lauriston, two important events took
place – the first Founders' Day celebration and the first
performance of Margaret Sommerville's play 'Mary

Margaret Sommerville

Erskine', the one following immediately on the other. A year later the pattern of Founders' Day was set for posterity:

> Founders' Day was celebrated in the school hall on the morning of 4th June. The deep yellow of the emblematic broom and the brilliant hoods of academic dress gave colour to the scene. The banner stood in its appointed place. Several distinguished former pupils were present and the Master of the Merchant Company and the Convener attended in their robes of office. Miss Clarke read the beautiful opening prayer for Founders' Day; the Master and the Senior Prefect Kathie Gower read, the pupils sang the Te Deum with fine effect and the whole assembly joined heartily in the 121st Psalm and the triumphant 'For all the Saints'. Dr.Strachan concluded [his address] by urging the pupils to weave characters which should be, like Mary Erskine's tapestry, 'sound in fabric, exquisite in design and fresh in colour.' It struck the inevitable note for Founders' Day, our debt to the past.[10]

The broad framework remains, only minor details have changed. The first Friday in June was for generations of girls a red-letter day, starting from their arrival at school an hour later than usual, hair brushed and braided, uniform immaculate. From the early days broom blossom figured largely as a decorative motif. Associated alike with the Erskines of Mar and with old Merchant Company tradition, it was also as a flower dear to Mary

The School Song

Clarke, who as a child remembered that 'for Queen Victoria's Jubilee all the front windows of the house and school were festooned with red blankets and masses of yellow broom'. The tradition grew that the classrooms should be decorated with flowers for Founders' Day, so Edinburgh gardens were scoured for the essential yellow sprays and for anything else that an early Scots summer could provide. Drooping lupins and magenta ponticums were combined with Solomon's Seal and crammed into vases and jam-jars on any available flat surface. Then it was down to the Hall and the joy of studying the outfits of the distinguished visitors before the Founders' Day hymn brought everyone to their feet for

Our Father by whose servants
This house was built of old.

There was a deliciously sad bit in the middle:

They reap not where they laboured,
We reap what they have sown.
Our harvest will be gathered
By ages not our own.

And then it was into the triumphant conclusion:

Before us and beside us
Still holden in Thy hand,
A cloud unseen of witness
Our elder comrades stand.
One family unbroken
We join with one acclaim
One heart, one voice uplifting
To glorify Thy name.

Then the Founders' Day prayer, remembering 'The Merchants of Edinburgh and Mary Erskine', the reading from Ecclesiasticus and the longueurs of the address by a Company representative, a public figure or a distinguished former pupil. Then with a final burst of sound in Miss Ferrier's school song, to music by Arthur Somervell –

Play the game nor heed the scar,
Hark! the slogan of the clans,
Erskine, Hopetoun, Marischal, Mar,
Mitis et Fortis!

– the school would pour out of the Hall to the stirring sound of the traditional march for a glorious afternoon of holiday.

The recollection of a historic past, the religious content of the service, the familiar music, the presence of Company members and distinguished former pupils, the clan structure and the motto were all part of Mary Clarke's legacy to the School. She had strong backing for this from many of her staff and especially from Mary Tweedie who would succeed her as Head and from Margaret Sommerville who was to write the first official School history as well as the 'Mary Erskine' play, first presented by the Former Pupils in 1922 and revived in 1935. Showing scenes from Mary Erskine's life and the early days of the Merchant Maiden Hospital with opportunities for a large cast of all ages from former pupils to small children, it was an unforgettable experience for audiences and actors alike.

Music and drama were also seen as important to the School's corporate identity. 'Music' of a sort there was, under the direction of James Moonie from 1889 to 1919. A stern disciplinarian with a short fuse, he still had the gift of inspiring his pupils, and the College's choral singing at Exhibitions and in public performances had a high reputation. Piano playing must have been a constant background to teaching at both Queen Street and George Square, for until 1924 seven hundred and fifty-eight girls had compulsory piano lessons. It was with relief that this system was ended with a considerable reduction in the size of the Music departments and with piano now being taught only to those with ability and interest. But there was as yet no orchestra, and school music was limited to choral and solo piano work. Drama productions were also limited by the lack of a stage. Once this had been built in 1921, more ambitious productions were possible, but apart from the 'Mary Erskine' play those in the early 1920s were limited to 'Scenes from' productions — 'Much Ado', 'Cranford' and 'The Life of Burns.' School societies, however, did provide a new dimension for the life of many girls which was often limited to home, school and church. A Literary and Dramatic Society had been formed in 1911; its programmes by the 1920s were predictably devoted to debates, lantern lectures and 'Parody Nights', though there is a delightful period flavour to one 1923 meeting:

> The 'Modern Night' which was a novelty consisted of a discussion of the merits and demerits of various modern celebrities; the classification was as follows; Geniuses: Barrie, Kipling, Wells and Lloyd George, Not: E. M. Dell, Angela Brazil, G. B. Shaw, A. S. M. Hutchinson, Meredith and Charlie Chaplin.[11]

Popular with all ages was the Field Club, founded in 1920, which offered not only lectures but the opportunity to get out into the countryside. It was the heir of the nineteenth-century Botanical Club which had offered its members an annual prize for the largest and most beautifully presented collection of dried flowers; collections of between one thousand and sixteen hundred specimens had not been unusual in those leisured days, but the Field Club was more active, visiting paper factories, rubber and chemical works, attending lectures on 'Alcohol' (with experiments) and 'a day out at Gullane where (tell it not in Gath!) we are perhaps to be regaled with ice-cream bricks!' The first Guide Company, founded in 1920 with sixteen members, rapidly extended to two and then three companies. Another surprisingly popular club was the Mission Settlement for University Women which had been founded in the 1880s and supported a Women's Mission in Bombay as well as providing lectures on and raising money for mission activities generally. Charitable effort was always part of the School's life. A Social Services Club was begun in 1920 with the aim of giving voluntary help to local organisations; under its auspices senior girls worked in

'Cranford'

local play-centres. A year or two later it was followed by an active Charities Committee. A link was formed in 1920 with a school at Seraincourt in the Ardennes and gifts of clothing, toys and books were sent, money was raised in sales to help Russian famine victims and areas of France which had suffered in the war, and for a time 'a Russian orphan was supported in Constantinople'. Local charities, however, had constant support through the small fund-raising efforts which have always been a part of School life.

During the war years and in the early 1920s any expansion of sport had been made very difficult because of the limited facilities and lack of space at Falconhall. The Field was shared with the George Square girls and was more convenient for a school which drew its pupils largely from the South Side. Queen Street girls tended to live to the north or outside the city because of the convenience of the railways, and a journey back from Morningside at the end of a strenuous afternoon was exhausting. Also there was no room there for the younger pupils whose only sport facility was basket ball. The Heads of both the Ladies' Colleges pressurised the Board and in 1920 plans were drawn up for a new Ladies' College Field at the junction of Ferry Road and East Fettes Avenue. This was opened on Founders' Day in 1923:

In the late afternoon of 4th June, 1923, a gay procession of girls wearing Queen Street colours might have been seen making its way down Ferry Road; by five o'clock a considerable number had assembled. Did ever tennis courts look over so glorious a stretch of country? Who would not barter the beeches of Falconhall for the prospect of the

Above *The old Field at Falconhall* Below *The new Field at Inverleith*

towering Pentlands and of mist-clothed Edinburgh? The ceremony was simple and dignified. Miss Clarke expressed as excellently as mere words could our abundant thanks
to the Merchant Company. With what rapt eyes did we watch her serve the first ball
on our own courts![12]

Tennis, hockey and netball facilities were now available and a popular swimming club
operated at Warrender Baths where many girls took life-saving courses. Golf was also
played, with an annual match between staff and pupils. School teams were now divided
into clan groups which stimulated competition. Inverleith field certainly extended the
school's sporting life; but many girls were daunted by the long journey back into town in
the late afternoon, struggling with heavy book bags and sports gear.

These developments did a great deal to enrich the girls' lives, but for the parents the
School's most important role was to educate. The post-war years saw a huge extension in
job opportunities for women in fields which their mothers would never had dreamed of,
and the Heads of the two Company Ladies' Colleges were careful to provide training facilities to suit the abilities of their wide range of pupils. Clerical courses with Spanish or
Russian were being offered as early as 1916; by 1920 a Post-Intermediate Art course was
operating and Greek was introduced in 1922 to supplement the School's reputation in
Latin teaching. The same year saw changes in the Scottish examination system with the
end of the old 'qualifying' and Intermediate certificates and the introduction of two
Secondary courses, a practical one for early leavers and one for Certificate pupils, very
much at the discretion of school Heads. Miss Clarke was aware of the needs of the School's
less academic girls and by the time of her retirement the Inspectors were giving high praise

to the work of the Domestic Science and Commercial departments, to 'basket-making, pottery, leather and bead-work' in the Art Department and to 'the making of wireless sets' in Science. At the same time the Higher Certificate leavers were following in the footsteps of their grandmothers who had left the College in the early days for degree courses. The pattern had been set in the 1880s:

Above *Hockey team* Below *Views of the Field*

Our old girls easily took first places in the University Local Examinations. In one year Annie Ferrier, Jessie Barron and May Angus, all now members of our staff, were the three first names on the list. They filled the University classes for women prior to 1892 [when] one of the first seven women to graduate M.A. was Flora Philip and one of the first to graduate in Medicine was also from Queen Street. Maria Ogilvie was the first woman D.Sc. of London University and Grace Masson probably the first Scotswoman

Art Class

to be head of an important English school [Middlesbrough High School for Girls].[13]

The star of these early academics was Ellen Higgins who had topped the London University matriculation list, gained a first-class in Mathematics at Oxford and as Principal of Royal Holloway College in the 1920s was a role model for all aspiring University entrants. A keen member of the Former Pupils' Guild, she visited the school regularly and backed Mary Clarke in her determination that clever girls could go south for degree courses as well as attending Scottish universities.

In 1924 Mary Clarke was asked to apply for the post of Headmistress of the Manchester High School for Girls and accepted it. She felt that her work at Queen Street was done; she could be proud of the school whose reputation as a flourishing and progressive body was largely due to her energy and determination, but she frankly acknowledged that there had been frustrations during her ten years in office:

> What tipped the scale for me was the unsatisfactory position of women in public life in Edinburgh and in Scotland generally. The Association of Headmistresses cut little ice in Scotland where co-educational schools under headmasters are the rule except in the largest cities. The Scots as a nation are less flexible than their southern neighbours and have continued to cling to a patriarchal pattern of society. England had far more to offer in educational opportunities than would ever have come my way had I remained in Scotland.[14]

Mary Clarke went on to a distinguished career in education in England, but returned to Edinburgh in her retirement and always retained a close link with her old school, serving for many years on the Merchant Company Education Board before her death in 1976. There were nineteen applications for her post, seven from England and five from school heads already in office. But the Board played safe; perhaps it was felt that things had been stirred up enough at Queen Street and that it was time to back-pedal a little. The appointment of Mary Tweedie, Head of the French department, was an in-house one in every

Juniors, 1914

sense for she had spent her life as one of the Family. Former pupil and bursar, Dux in 1894 with a distinguished academic record, she had spent the previous nineteen years on the staff at Queen Street, and her only experience outwith Edinburgh had been during her university years. At forty-eight she was the oldest of all the applicants; she was to be Head for the next thirteen years.

REFERENCES

1–3	CLARKE *A Short Life of Ninety Years.*
4	M.M. 1958.
5–6.	CLARKE, *op.cit.*
7	M.M. 1967.
8	CLARKE, *op.cit.*
9	M.M. 1920.
10	M.M. 1922.
11–12	M.M. 1923.
13	M.M. 1920.
14	CLARKE, *op.cit.*

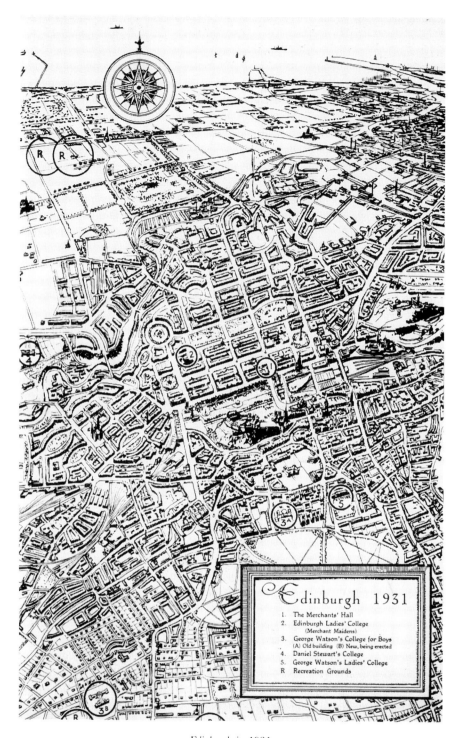

Edinburgh 1931

1. The Merchants' Hall
2. Edinburgh Ladies' College
   (Merchant Maidens)
3. George Watson's College for Boys
   (A) Old building (B) New, being erected
4. Daniel Stewart's College
5. George Watson's Ladies' College
R Recreation Grounds

Edinburgh in 1931

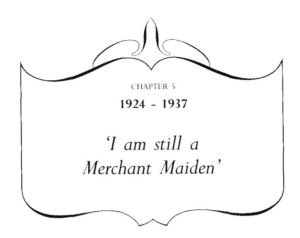

Mary Tweedie was introduced to the girls as their new Head at the Empire Day service in 1924. She was known to them all, not only as a dynamic teacher of languages but also as Editor of the 'Merchant Maiden' and a firm upholder of Queen Street's traditions. Under her calm direction the College would continue to prosper; it was at capacity in the year that she became Head with a roll of nine hundred and sixty-one, all under one roof in Queen Street since the return of the Elementary Department in 1921. On the surface Edinburgh life in the mid-'20s seemed settled and secure:

I came to the school when we still celebrated Empire Day, when the two-minute silence on Armistice Day descended on us like a cosmic hiatus, when authority in most forms was unquestioned, when the moral code was fixed, when we could think of ourselves as Merchant Maidens without coyness, when unlike Miss Jean Brodie's créme de la créme the only Spanish war any of us heard of would be the Peninsular campaign and our Biology lessons were strictly about flowers, birds and bees. We called our mums mummies then.[1]

Mary Tweedie

The Well

The Hall

The Refectory

The Roof Garden

But the stresses were there, if not for the girls at least for their parents, the school staff and the Education Board. The Queen Street building was grossly overcrowded; dinners (66,000 during the session) had to be eaten in two shifts and there was a desperate lack of space for midday recreation. The old building was well beyond its sell-by date and was shabby and inconvenient. Major improvements were made in 1927:

> The fully equipped additional gymnasium, the installation of electric light throughout the old building and the complete removal of galleries from the junior classrooms have been of considerable benefit, but this emphasises the poor ventilation in the old building and the need for modern seating and equipment.[2]

In her report the following year Mary Tweedie again drew the Board's attention to the need to modernise the building:

> The progressive redecoration of the school is gradually bringing it into line with modern needs. The ventilation of the older parts of the building is unpleasantly inadequate and there is a real need for modern seating and equipment. The heavy old-fashioned benches are quite beyond the strength of the junior pupils and the desks nailed to the floor are condemned by all modern regulations. The effete equipment is largely in those portions of the school overlooking Queen Street where the ever-growing noise of traffic is a threat to the nervous stability of the pupils. There have been two severe cases of nervous break-down in pupils transferred from country schools. I would urge upon the Education Board the grave nature of the problem, more especially in view of the recent proposal made in the Edinburgh Town Council to divert further heavy traffic along Queen Street.[3]

The problem of noise in the classrooms facing Queen Street had been under constant discussion for over thirty years. The Board could do no more here than present its annual petitions to the Town Council for the laying of deadening wood blocks to replace cobbles. It did however act on the replacement of furnishings and on some decoration of the shabbier parts of the building; in 1929 Mary Tweedie was grateful for

> the freshness and renewed beauty of the Hall which has given daily pleasure; the Board has also undertaken the provision of modern desks for the older portion of the building.[4]

The new furniture costing £420, just under £2 for each desk and chair, was duly installed; the old pieces were sold as scrap, totalling twelve tons of desk tops and four and a half tons of desk frames along with three hundredweight of old light fittings. The Board further improved the Hall by installing

> several old mirrors, the property of the original Merchant Maiden Hospital with a suitable inscription in the Assembly Hall.[5]

These had been removed from the Lauriston building, sold for demolition to the Infirmary Board after the removal of George Watson's College to Colinton Road. The Education Board had more sense of history and of architectural heritage than their 1967 successors who saw this same Hall, with its fine decorative features including these mirrors, reduced to rubble in the demolition of the Queen Street building.

Year by year the Inspectors commented on the noise, crowding and inconvenience in the building but nothing was done. In the economic climate of the early 1930s the Board, fully stretched after the building of the new George Watson's, had no funds to spare. The recession years affected the College resources also. In 1932 Mary Tweedie noted that the annual trip to France had been cancelled and that

> The present economic climate is reflected in the reduced number of school dinners, six thousand less being served, and the reduced number taking a prolonged training after leaving school. Fewer former pupils are entering the Universities except for Honours degrees; these number twelve as against twenty entering the College of Domestic Science.[6]

In 1933 'the economic situation is reflected in the increasing number of pupils desiring to prepare for various branches of the Civil service', and a year later there was

> a marked anxiety about future occupations. Fathers have appeared more willing to have their daughters trained for their own professions. Universities attract many, but our pupils show a greater preference for degrees with Honours [and] suffer little from unemployment.[7]

The bias towards practical careers in this period of unemployment was noticeable; science-based training in pharmacology, dietetics, radiography and biochemical research was becoming popular, along with banking and library training and the traditional career options of teaching, law, nursing and domestic science.

Mary Tweedie was aware of the need to provide a curriculum to satisfy the needs of these pupils. She was not happy with the new examination regulations, regretting the old Intermediate Certificate and feeling that the new Higher Day School Certificate was

> not suited to our type of school. The compulsion to continue all certificate subjects until the final year results in a very regrettable lack of freedom to adjust courses in view of special ability. The withdrawal of the privilege to concentrate on the chief subjects of the course in the last years is a distinct blow to the finest work of the secondary school. I hope in consultation with my staff to put before the Education Board proposals to cease presenting for this certificate and to substitute a certificate of our own which shall be at least equal in standard to the old Intermediate. A Leaving Certificate course has been prepared and provisionally approved by the S.E.D.[8]

A Senior Class

This course would include Domestic Science and Commercial options. In 1926 a post-leaving course in Higher Physics was introduced for university candidates and successful presentations were made the following year in both Higher Physics and Biology. For younger pupils 'everyday Science' was available in Year I and the Inspectors approved 'the direct teaching of hygiene' throughout the school.

The annual Reports on the successes of former pupils remained consistently impressive. In 1931 three full pages of close print in the prospectus detailed forty-three 'Degrees, Diplomas and other distinctions gained at Edinburgh University and elsewhere', including three Doctorates as well as seven class prizes and medals gained at Edinburgh University, numerous class certificates in a wide range of Science and Arts subjects and certification in Art, Accountancy and Domestic Sciences. It is perhaps significant that, with the exception of students attending foreign universities as part of a language course, these pupils were almost all attending the local University. A year later, in 1932, major awards were given to leavers at Girton and Somerville but this was unusual; there was less impetus from school or parents to send daughters to English or even to Scottish universities other than Edinburgh, possibly a reflection of the need for economy in a period of recession. By now an impressive list of prizes was available for presentation at the annual Usher Hall Exhibition and Prize-giving, the names of many of them reflecting former pupils, staff and Merchant Company officials who had gifted them; affection, loyalty, gratitude, grief are all bound up with names familiar to the prizewinners of the 1990s – Brand, Glass, Ferrier,

MITIS ET FORTIS

THE MARY ERSKINE SCHOOL

Coat of Arms of The Mary Erskine School

Aerial view of the School in its new home at Ravelston

The School seen from the playing fields

A direct link with Mary Erskine − the 1710 table carpet made for the
Governors of the Merchant Maiden Hospital

The Tercentenary Mural, designed and made by Margery Clinton, presented to the School by the Former Pupils Guild, and unveiled by Her Majesty the Queen on 30th June 1994

The School Staff, summer 1994

Three Principals of The Mary Erskine School:
(left) Patrick Tobin (1989 -), Jean Thow (1967 - 1978) and Robin Morgan (1978 - 1989)

School pupils model the Tercentenary tartan

Wider horizons: a visit to Rome in the 1970s

1981: Her Majesty the Queen and pupils, with the Master of the Merchant Company, admire one of the embroideries made by pupils and staff and presented to the Merchant Company on the occasion of its Tercentenary.

Her Majesty the Queen, accompanied by the Duke of Edinburgh and the Senior Prefect,
visits the School on 30th June 1994. In the background, Secretary of State for Scotland Ian Lang and Master of
the Merchant Company James Miller. On the wall, paintings by pupils of former School buildings.
In the centre, the School's second home at Bristo.

Mitchell, Kirk Mackie, Fraser – though sadly today's stars in Mathematics and History no longer receive the gold watch, bracelet or brooch that were once gifted by George Watson's and Daniel Stewart's. The years 1934 and 1935 saw two generous endowments in medicine and law bursaries by one of the original pupils, Lady Steele, in memory of her sister who had been Dux in 1871; these commemorated the School's 250th anniversary and were typical of the strong sense of loyalty and affection felt for it by its former pupils. The annual Prize-giving in the Usher Hall and the biennial Exhibitions of work at the School continued to attract great interest and were fully reported in the Press; in 1929 a curious instant tradition was introduced which does not seem to have had a long life:

> The Gymnastic Exhibitions were performed to crowded audiences and contained various new features, including the 'tossing-out' of leaving pupils according to the traditions of the English public schools.[9]

While 1933 saw

> a series of large posters illustrative of Whipsnade and various railway and business enterprises; the Science department demonstrated how to make bath crystals and boot blacking. Some hundreds of summer frocks, dressing gowns, overalls, pyjamas and other garments made by the pupils were displayed and some presented in a march past.[10]

The Elementary and Junior departments also held Exhibitions along with small plays and dance demonstrations, reported with great coyness; an obsession with flower fairies, snowflakes and small furry animals marks all reports of activity at this end of the School.

Mary Tweedie and Staff

The "Tail" of a Visit to the Junior School

With apologies to " Alice in Wonderland "

The blood-thirsty five graders
cut up bull's eyes and learn about
animals' hearts, brains and ears ; use
poster-paints ; write French plays ;
make lino-cuts ; fr m big charts on
the walls learn Geog. without tears.
They have sections at gym.; dance
'Scottish Reform': analysing is child's
play to the Fifth Form. The four
grade has started geology now;
make plays from their reading; do
fractions with ease ; Coronation
designs for gay cushions they plan;
collect labels from countries far over
the seas; on gym days right up to the
rope-tops they race, each striving hard
that her clan may gain first place.
The three grade know heraldry,
paint coats-of-arms ; watch growing bean seeds, know the names of each
part; dance the turning waltz properly;
draw such neat maps, and know lots of
long poems right off by heart. They
don't like long money sums—that they
admit, but exams never worry the three
grade a bit. Though the two
grade are smaller they too
climb the ropes, and know
many strange things about
birds and rabbits. They told
us of Eskimoes, with husky
dogs, of Arabs, and High-
landers and their strange
habits. They dance waltzes
and polkas; *they're* not dull
and staid, but as learned as
their elders, the busy two
grade. Grade one's rooms
are like gardens all full of
fresh flowers they
grow these themselves,
know all of their names, but
they're practical too. knit
a blanket all shades, and
show us press-cuttings
and pictures in frames.
On their traycloths
they grow marigolds.
sweet peas, roses; we
eft with the sweet
scent of flowers
in our
noses. K. H.; I. W.

The 'Tail' of a visit to the Junior School

Various important anniversaries marked the early 1930s and provided opportunities for a varied range of celebrations. 1931 saw the 250th anniversary of the founding of the Merchant Company and was marked in December by two performances of a commemorative Masque in the Usher Hall, presented by all the Company schools. The Ladies' College contribution was an adaptation by Margaret Sommerville from her earlier 'Mary Erskine' play; using scenes featuring the Foundress and members of the Merchant Company, it provided thirty-six acting roles for the girls as well as parts for younger children in the Prologue and Epilogue. 1934 saw the College's own 240th anniversary, marked by a special Service at Greyfriars

to commemorate its long connection with the Merchant Maidens who worshipped there until 1870. There are still alive Merchant Maidens who sat in the gallery with the boys from George Watson's Hospital opposite and from George Heriot's in the gallery opposite to the pulpit. The pupils down to 4 Junior were present and the church was crowded with friends of the School, including one family which represented three generations of Merchant Maidens. The Rev. Dr.W. W. Gardiner, Minister of Greyfriars' Church, officiated and the Master of the Merchant Company, the Headmistress, the President of the Former Pupils' Club and the senior Prefect took part in the service. Among others present were Bailie Easterbrook representing the Lord Provost, the

Anniversary Service

Treasurer of the Merchant Company, besides representatives of ancient benefactions dating back to the end of the seventeenth century. Many kind messages were received from representatives of ancient benefactions, from city guilds and corporations, from donors of endowed prizes, from the London and Glasgow Clubs, from former members of staff and from other friends including one who was a pupil before 1870 at Lauriston. We would mention the messages from the Earl of Mar and Kellie whose family, as representing Mary Erskine, have presented continuously since 1696 four foundationers to the School.

The address was given by Miss M.G. Clarke, Headmistress of Manchester High School for Girls and formerly Headmistress of the Edinburgh Ladies' College, who said that this was above all an occasion for looking at once backward and forward and quoted from Miss Sommerville's play 'Mary Erskine'; 'I would like to see the lasses of simple taught as well as the daughters of gentle. Education is a blessing that should be common to all.'[11]

The occasion, bringing together large numbers of former pupils, staff and friends, was a happy one; a year later the Former Pupils' Guild celebrated its own fiftieth birthday with a second performance of the 'Mary Erskine' play, still vivid in the memory of those who took part in it. By now the school had more dramatic skills available, largely due to the fact that footlights and curtains had been provided for the stage in the Hall and perfor-

The Commemorative Masque, 1931

Coronation Pageant, 1937

mances of 'Quality Street', 'The Glen is Mine' and 'Will Shakespeare' could be given; £20 from the profits of 1927's main performance went to the appeal for the new Shakespeare Theatre at Stratford. Pageants also seem to have been a feature of this period, with one for a royal visit at Craigmillar Castle in 1927, a League of Nations Pageant by local schools in 1930 and a 'Coronation pageant and playlet by the babies' in 1937. In contrast the School's music remained rather static. The 1929 Usher Hall prize-giving revived as a one-off the old tradition of playing on six pianos; in 1934 a special report on Music in the Merchant Company schools showed three hundred Ladies' College girls still taking piano lessons, more than half of them being taught in pairs, and a large Music staff. The following year the Inspector praised the 'virility, a feature of the highest classes in their choral work' under Dr.Greenhouse Allt, but by then the orchestra, only formed in 1933, had found its feet. Made up entirely of string players, it numbered thirteen girls and five members of staff, including the multi-talented Margaret Sommerville. It had a short life, proving impossible to maintain during the disruptions of the war years.

When Mary Tweedie became Head the popularity of sport was shown in the membership of the Clubs — two hundred and ten in Hockey, well over three hundred in Tennis, almost a hundred for Swimming at George Watson's or Warrender Baths and even fifty for Cricket; by 1926 Netball was another popular option. There were still annual charges for the use of the Field, a five-shilling flat rate with supplements of one shilling for winter and half-a-crown for summer games, while the Juniors had no Field facilities

The first Orchestra

Hockey team

until 1929; in that year they were being bussed down to Inverleith, but their elders either took the Goldenacre tram or walked by Church Lane and Comely Bank — pleasant going down but killing coming up again. The Clans continued to compete in sport and now had a Trophy embroidered with the Company arms which had been presented by the Head, and they had laid out Clan gardens at the Field Gate. By the 1930s with Miss Park, herself a notable international hockey player in charge of Physical Education, sport had reached a very high standard and the School was unbeatable in hockey, winning the Edinburgh Schools' Challenge Shield three years running, coming top as the best School Life-Saving team in the Empire and providing the winner of the National Golf Championship Cup. The Inspectors were impressed by the outdoor sport facilities but continued to be appalled by those for indoor Physical Education:

> The two gymnasia are under street level, considerably under standard dimensions and badly ventilated; however the work of the pupils especially in Dancing is to be commended.[12]

School Societies continued very much in the pattern set by Mary Clarke and give the impression of being worthy and uninspired. The Field Club had one unusual outing in 1926 when they went to stay at Polam Hall in Yorkshire to view a total eclipse of the sun, but the normal offerings were visits to Gas Works, lectures on Bees and debates on 'Woman's Place is the Home'. Charitable efforts were more imaginative; in 1925 the Charities' Committee, now extended to the Junior School, organised a Self-denial Week, raising £9.10.212 by various efforts:

> Many saved car [tram] fares by walking to and from school; one girl denied herself tennis to which she goes by car four times. Real self-denial is clearly seen in the purchase of a 2d instead of a 3d ice-cream.[13]

When the fuel shortage caused by the General Strike closed Warrender Baths in 1926, the swimmers gave their Club fee to charity, toys and books were brought every Christmas to Craiglockhart Poorhouse, books were donated to the University Settlement, and for several years 'a large number of used magazines was collected for the navvies at Baddingsgill Reservoir'. The annual picnic in the King's Park was given for the children of the Cowgate Sabbath Morning Free Breakfast Mission and the Grassmarket Child Garden received 'golliwogs, whips, balls, linen scrap-books, carts made from cigar boxes, dolls' houses and babies' jackets'. In all this the School continued its long tradition of supporting Edinburgh children in need, but in 1932 when money was tight Mary Tweedie commented on 'the multiplicity of small efforts needed to maintain our social welfare work'.

One feature of the post-war years from the mid-'20s was the opportunity for foreign travel, with an annual trip to France arranged by the Modern Language department with Mary Tweedie's enthusiastic backing. In pre-war days the links with Europe had been in Germany; in 1908 'E.K.R.' had reported in the 'Merchant Maiden':

In Hildesheim we pass a school which has a special interest for us, so many of our friends have studied there including five of our Duxes. The first of our girls went in 1881 and since then there has been an almost unbroken list of former pupils. No wonder our old school is well known there; did not one of our old girls mark out the first school tennis-court? The whole school got a half-holiday to watch the first lesson and 'Tennis' was put in the time-table. Another of our girls tried to start 'Hockey' but that was considered too unladylike; the Principal of the school asked if it would not be a better game if everyone had a ball.[14]

Germany, however, for economic and emotional reasons, was no longer a popular school trip option, but France was ideal, cheap, safely different and providing good opportunities for language study. Most years between 1926 and 1935 between twenty and thirty seniors travelled to Paris, Brittany, Tours or Alsace with Miss Laurenson or Miss Sommerville in charge. In 1933

Many friends, amongst whom was Miss Tweedie and a little dog wearing the school colours in our honour, saw us off at Waverley; twenty-six hours later we were in Strasbourg. We were most comfortably housed in the Cercle Evangelique; in our charming study-bedrooms we slept and talked most satisfactorily and in the salon des dames of an evening we did a little sewing or knitting and much dancing of Scottish reels for the entertainment of other guests or even of the street. Our days were so full of pleasure in the seeing of things new and fascinating that we could fill a special issue of the 'Merchant Maiden' with our memories.[15]

Many of Mary Tweedie's pupils still living have vivid recollections of Queen Street sixty or seventy years ago. They remember as Juniors their classrooms at the top of the building and being led down the long flights of 'splintery' stairs hand-in-hand with the Prefects for fire-drills; the whole school lined up in form order along the pavement. One five-year-old walked daily from Wardie to Queen street and remembered in 1926 being held up by a strikers' demonstration at the Hanover Street crossing; one of the men carried her across on his shoulder, calling 'Way for a leddy gaun to the skule', and carried her back on her way home.

Once a month the Juniors had Shield Day, signalled by the singing of 'Onward Christian Soldiers' at their assembly and the presentation for the most deserving form, not necessarily for academic merit.

Clothes figure large in their memories; the uniform list was staggering and must have represented a very large outlay for a family with no older sisters or cousins to hand things on. The school pupil of the '30s dressed from the skin out in a vest, a liberty bodice, navy bloomers (worn for gym), black stockings held up with suspenders or garters, a gym slip (but seniors wore skirts), white blouse with tie and square-necked blouses for gym and games. Over all this went a navy melton cloth coat or a gaberdine (both were obligatory) worn with a velour hat or a navy woollen cap for cold weather which could pull down to cover the ears. Brown leather gloves were always worn and black laced shoes; in your slipper bag you carried strapped house shoes, gym shoes, dancing pumps and games shoes or boots. Summer saw blazers and panamas with sprigged Tobralco dresses, pink, blue or green; gloves had to be worn in the summer too and were always worn in dancing class; the Juniors still wore pinafores. The high spot of the end of the summer holidays was the visit to one of the city's school outfitters (Jenners had the arms of all its customer schools round the school department walls), followed by a trip to Thin's or Baxendine's to buy books; these were brought home and covered in new crisp brown paper held down with sealing-wax and neatly lettered on the cover. For prize-givings and concerts white dresses were worn with silk stockings and dancing pumps.

In Mary Tweedie's day there were sixty women on the staff and only eight men; this, and the fact that women staff were generally unmarried, reflected the destruction of young life in the War. The staff were seen by their pupils as utterly dedicated to the School and to them; they set very high standards in work, behaviour, manners and punctuality and the girls were reminded that the School's good name depended on their behaviour at all times. Women teachers were important role models in the days before television; their clothes and hair-styles were often elegant and much admired. It was of course obligatory to have crushes on one or other of the male staff, however old they were. Discipline was built in and was maintained at all times, even on the occasion when a ball came bouncing down the dining-room stairs from Junior recreation in the hall above and plopped splashily straight into a bowl of soup. Prize-givings are vividly remembered: the lining up of the forms on the Usher Hall stairs, the synchronised marching in to the organ gallery to Miss Badger's school march on the organ, the solemn moment when the Banner was carried onto the stage by the Senior Prefect, its supporting cords held by the Games Captain and the Dux. The Dux's great moment came as the culmination of the prize-giving; she generally had quite a pile of prizes and it was not considered suitable for her to carry them off herself, so she made her curtsey and walked off empty-handed, followed by the Janitor carrying her trophies for her. Both James and his successor Henry wore tail-coats and Henry had a distinct swagger on stage which caused great joy.

In 1937 Mary Tweedie announced her retirement at the end of a year that the 'Merchant Maiden' described as 'almost unique in our long record'. Ellen Higgins, one of the original Lauriston girls, had been the Founders' Day speaker, paying tribute to the legacy of Mary Erskine and the school's four Heads. The Coronation and a royal visit to Edinburgh had meant holidays, processions and participation in royal events; the Guides had helped to form a guard of honour at the State Entry and many pupils had taken part in a Youth Rally and in keep-fit demonstrations for the monarchs. 'We are reminded', said the editor, 'of the day in 1841 when Merchant Maidens took part in the welcome to Queen Victoria on a special stand in the Royal Mile.'

In her farewell to her pupils Mary Tweedie looked back on her years as pupil, teacher and Head of the school, reminding them that

the building has changed out of all recognition. The curriculum is far different and immeasurably wider. We require no longer to seek like Dr. Pryde 'to teach girls all that

Art Students

men are taught.' Yet I see no fundamental change in the pulsing life that calls down to my room from the Roof Garden or bubbles in happy laughter from the class-rooms. It existed already in the days of David Pryde and of Ellen Higgins. The young Victorian played the same human pranks. The spirit of adventure lives still. I rejoice that I belong to a school that links up what is best from all classes of the community. I rejoice in the traditions of the School and of the Merchant Company; in the countless Merchant Maidens I know and love here and in many other countries; in the thought of parents whose fine cooperation has made my own task light; in the memory of a splendid staff,

Art Exhibition including the Banner

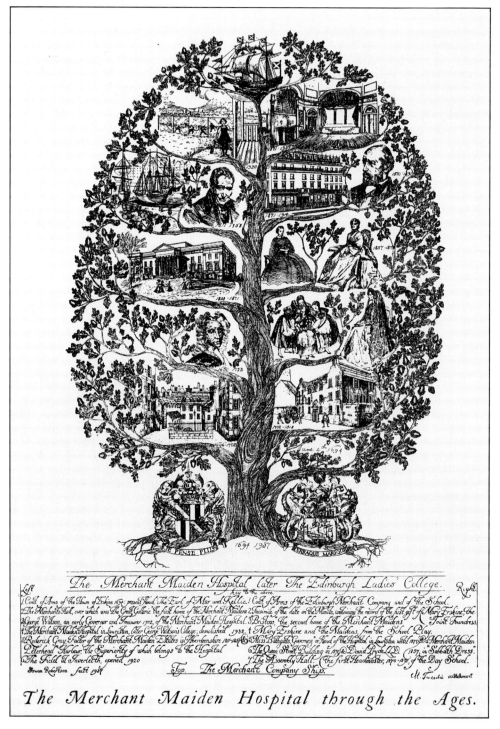

The Merchant Maiden Hospital (later The Edinburgh Ladies' College).

The Merchant Maiden Hospital through the Ages.

Mary Tweedie's Tree

loyal and ungrudging. I do not say goodbye but farewell. I am still a Merchant Maiden and I send to you all the message of affection that joins friends of all ages.[16]

Mary Clarke's leaving gift to the school had been a terracotta kneeling figure of a girl. Regrettably covered in paint by a later generation, today it faces Mary Tweedie's gift, an illustrated Family Tree of the School from its foundation, inscribed 'The Merchant Maiden Hospital through the Ages'. It was characteristic of her love of the school and of its past that she would commission this; it was equally characteristic of her love for her girls that every one of them would receive a copy of the Tree, personally signed by their Headmistress.

REFERENCES

1   MURIEL MCNAUGHTON.
2   PRINCIPAL'S REPORT, 1927.
3   PRINCIPAL'S REPORT, 1928.
4   PRINCIPAL'S REPORT, 1929.
5   M.M.H.M. DECEMBER, 1929.
6   PRINCIPAL'S REPORT, 1932.
7   PRINCIPAL'S REPORT, 1933.
8   PRINCIPAL'S REPORT, 1925.
9   PRINCIPAL'S REPORT, 1929.
10 PRINCIPAL'S REPORT, 1933.
11 M.M., 1934.
12 INSPECTORS' REPORT, 1934.
13 M.M., 1925.
14 M.M., 1908.
15 M.M., 1933.
16 M.M., 1937.

Marjorie Chaplyn

The advertisement of the post of Headmistress of the Ladies' College attracted twenty-two applicants, many of them former pupils of the Company's girls' schools. Fifteen applications were received from English candidates and seven from Headmistresses already in post; but again the Board's choice fell on a former pupil. Marjorie Chaplyn, Dux in 1916, went on to graduate at Edinburgh with first-class honours in Latin and French and to take the teacher's training certificate at St.George's College which led her to teaching posts in Manchester and Edinburgh. In 1925 she began work for a doctorate at the Sorbonne, and after completing it went on to further teaching and to a post as Lecturer in Education at King's College, London. As well as being a considerable French scholar, she was deeply interested in theological study and at the time of her appointment at the age of thirty-eight had almost completed the course for the Lambeth Diploma. Many years later she would be remembered for 'her striking good looks, her beautiful voice, commanding presence, great kindness and ready sympathy and for her wit, gaiety and charm'. She had the gift of inspiring warm affection in her colleagues and her pupils, had a deep love of the School and its traditions and considerable experience in the world of education. It was her misfortune to take up her post as Headmistress a year before the rumbling of imminent war began to be felt, to have to steer the school through disruption and upheaval in 1939 and to know that the building which housed her pupils and staff was not only inconvenient and shabby but a death-trap in the event of enemy action from the air.

The session which ended in the summer of 1938 was the last normal one which the school would enjoy for a generation of girls. The Merchant Company held celebrations for its 240th anniversary and, to mark the occasion, handed over to the College several pieces which had until then been kept at the Hall — the portrait of James Pryde by his son, antique chests and a set of Hepplewhite chairs. It was an open secret that the Hammond organ, presented in the autumn for use at Assembly, was a leaving gift from Margaret Sommerville; the Former Pupils had already donated a handsome lectern for the Hall. 1938 was the year of the Glasgow International Exhibition and the Company marked this by commissioning a film about its Schools from Campbell Harper; made at

Marjorie Chaplyn and the Prefects

A Junior Pageant

a cost of £25, it was mainly devoted to the boys' Colleges, but had some 'shots of the Ladies' Colleges on the playing field'.

Marjorie Chaplyn did what she could to make the old building workable and comfortable. New desks and filing cabinets were installed and the Inspectors commented approvingly:

> The new Headmistress has successfully planned some minor improvements. The Hall when not in use for examination purposes will be made to accommodate two classes; improved library accommodation will be ready next session, the present library room being transformed into a class-room and an additional room for Art will be provided. It is also anticipated that new equipment will be available for laundry work and increased accommodation for the teaching of science.[1]

But they were less happy about the Elementary department, dangerously housed on the top floor of the old building, and were critical as ever of the unsatisfactory gymnasium facilities, 'but the girls do manage to change into bright modern gymnastic dress and show a responsive attitude to the subject'. Impressed by the considerable interest taken on the games field, they noted: 'on occasion the field is hardly sufficient to cope with the numbers taking part'.[2]

Staff / Pupils golf match

At the Prize-giving of 1938 farewells were said to two long-standing members of staff. Jessie Graham retired after thirty-nine years of teaching dancing to her 'naughty darlings', as did Elizabeth Reid, a former pupil, Senior Assistant under the three previous Heads, Deputy in absence for both Mary Clarke and Mary Tweedie and the efficient power behind the throne in running the school. One medallist, however, was absent and still wonders whether she made the right decision in passing up her great day. With a group of girls from Scottish schools she had sailed to Canada, a visit arranged by Mary Tweedie after her visit there in 1931 with a group of Headmistresses which included Mary Clarke. (The Canadian visit was to be repeated with some drama the following year for another group of girls who, returning by liner in September, were turned back on the threat of submarine action and spent in some cases the duration of the war overseas.) For the girls ending the session in the summer of 1938 and looking forward to holidays, life in and out of school seemed normal and predictable. The Swimming Gala had been held at Dunbar; riding classes at Belford had been introduced and were popular. A third Guide Company had been formed, the School had presented 'Pygmalion' and Clan Mar had come out the winner in the Sports and been presented with 'a print of one of Dame Laura Knight's most beautiful pictures'.

Behind the scenes their elders at Merchants' Hall and in the Company Schools were not looking forward to a relaxed summer holiday; events in Europe were being anxiously watched and plans made for a situation which seemed unthinkable twenty years after the Armistice. In October 1938 the Education Board issued a memoradum prepared at the time of the Munich Conference:

A supply of chloride of lime for gas decontamination has been provided at each school and further equipment necessary is being ordered. At the Boys' schools sites for shelter trenches have been selected and picks and shovels have been provided. Should the Air Raid Precautions Committee so decide tomorrow, work on digging can proceed immediately. Corrugated iron for shelter in trenches is available and an option has been obtained on wood for revetting trenches where necessary. As regards the Edinburgh Ladies' College the Secretary has approached Queen Street Gardens Commissioners for permission to dig trenches there in the event of it being necessary to evacuate the school. The Secretary has arranged to address the Schools' staffs on gas decontamination and elementary First Aid in gas cases. The Committee might carefully consider whether in the event of war and the subsequent dislocation of services it might not be advisable to close the Schools for a week or ten days until the times become more normal. Mr.Sleigh has brought to the notice of the meeting the situation of the Primary department at Queen Street which is on the top flat of the building and has suggested that the closing down of this department might have to be seriously considered. Principal Smail of Heriot Watt College was unhappy about the slit trenches in the public gardens for the two girls' schools, for if a sudden emergency arose and the public ran indiscriminately for shelter, they would disregard any proprietary rights in trenches and the accommodation thought to be available for the girls might be found to be occupied by members of the public. The school buildings and their basements might prove death-traps, though it was thought that air-raids were more likely at night.[3]

The Munich agreement did little to reassure the Education Board; early in 1939, after approving designs for new summer dresses and prefects' ties, they were discussing the Government's evacuation plans and deciding that if the Company Schools were to be evacuated it must be as units; if children were absorbed separately or in small groups into rural authority schools, the Board would lose fee revenue. In July as the school session ended it was agreed that temporary slit trenches in George Square and Queen Street Gardens should be prepared and parents should be issued with the Board's proposals for the possible evacuation of the two girls' schools. The boys' colleges were considered far enough away from the city centre to be reasonably safe from air attack; but the girls' buildings were very central and Queen Street in particular was seen as a potential fire hazard. If war broke out the girls' schools were to close and each would be accommodated in its neighbouring boys' building; a shift teaching system would be introduced, morning and afternoon teaching to be alternated monthly between the children. Written work was to be set to be done at home and such peripheral subjects as Dancing, Music and Religious Education were to be removed from the timetable. Shelters would be built at the boys' schools and each parent would be asked to contribute 5/- towards their cost. No reduction in fees would be considered even with a shorter school day.

The autumn session of 1939 opened with the Queen Street building abandoned, all its treasures stored in the Merchants' Hall basement and a First Aid Post installed in the

Daniel Stewart's College.

building. The senior girls were initially sent written work to do at home which was post-ed back to staff for marking. They were then given instructions to attend their staggered classes at Daniel Stewart's, Queensferry Road, on the half-day shift system. The first day of its operation must have had much in common with the first day of the old Institution at Lauriston almost seventy years before. Not only Queen Street girls were being absorbed, but also some from George Watson's Ladies' College who would find travelling with wartime city transport difficult. Facilities were limited; all outer garments and the obliga-tory gasmasks were carried from room to room and draped over radiators or piled on the floor. Senior pupils had known for months that 'evacuation for the duration' to Daniel Stewart's was likely but had hoped that they would never find themselves there:

> The building is old and rather grey. At the foot of the first flight of steps is a memori-al commemorating those who were killed in the war of 1914—1918 and we remember that we are in the midst of another, a recollection which is confirmed by large unsight-ly mounds of earth under the trees. Great was the speculation that first morning. Of course the new school life was very different from what we had been accustomed to. The school hours made it difficult for us to get a meal in the middle of the day. Some rules were relaxed and new ones made. Periods were shorter and more work had to be got through. Many girls had left and new ones had come from other schools and above all the space in the actual building was rather limited. The first day back at School in normal circumstances is rather hilarious and we half feared that this one would be 'a riot' but in spite of the many gas-mask drills which we had, the School as a whole set-tled down very quickly. We grew accustomed to the new situation and there were many amusing diversions, such as the first occasion on which we had to use the Shelters seri-ously and, owing to the cement floors not being quite dry and hard, we had to keep moving our feet so as not to be cemented in.[4]

A fourth-year girl, set an essay on the Shift System, commented:

> The system is excellent when I come to School in the morning but when I have to come in the afternoon I think it is dreadful. The morning passes quickly and soon it is a quar-ter-past twelve. As we leave the grounds, thinking of dinner awaiting us and seeing the boys on their way to work, a smile finds its way to my face. Lessons are soon finished after dinner and then I am free.
> Although we have to go to School on Saturdays, after School is over for the day and homework finished we are free. Of the two shifts I prefer the morning shift. At first I did feel rather tired after getting up at a quarter to seven but once one is up it is delight-ful walking down a quiet road to a car stop before anyone else is awake.
> I don't like the system of a double shift in the least. I should like to be back in Queen Street, to know when I was going to School and when I was finished.[5]

With youth's resilience the girls and boys adjusted to the situation, but the strain on both staffs was considerable and many found the situation almost intolerable. Marjorie Chaplyn,

Finnish Relief Sale, 1940

suffering from a duodenal ulcer which would hospitalise her in the summer, still saw that everything was done to keep the pupils as busy and happy as was possible in the circumstances. In the spring of 1940 a Sale in aid of Finnish Relief provided a happy diversion:

Each clan was to display its wares on two tables covered with crepe paper in the Clan colour. Lessons only lasted for two periods that day and soon the moment arrived when Dr.Chaplyn declared the Sale open. The somewhat self-conscious helpers stood behind the stalls, their Clan-bands over their shoulders, while on the tables in front of them lay a treasure trove of knitted socks, scarves and gloves, exquisite hand-painted brooches and rings, dainty little matinee coats, a golden pyramid of oranges. We left School that night with a feeling of pride that Queen Street had 'done its bit' to help others whose misfortunes and hardships might so easily be our own.[6]

" Merchant Maiden " Competition

WE publish four of the Farewell Addresses to Stewart's sent in by competitors. The prize has been awarded to Margaret Howie, Va.

Farewell to Stewart's

(With abject apologies to Longfellow.)

IN the region of the North Wind,
Of the North West Wind, Keewaydin,
Stands a college, tall and stately,
Stands a college, grey and revered;
Turreted it is, and windowed,
And beloved of many pigeons;
Overlooking spacious gardens,
Staring out across the housetops,
Far across a sea of wigwams,
Farther yet across the river
To the hills of Fife beyond it,
To the mountains of the Northland;
And within its solemn portals
Boys were taught of art and learning,
Taught to deal with Mathematics,
Physics, Chemistry and Latin.
Happy were they in their college,
Happy in the days of peace-time,
Carried on their quiet studies,
Sought to better their instruction.

Came a time of mad confusion,
Of alarms and excursions,
Daily danger, nightly perils,
Time of war and time of air-raids.
Thrust aside and rendered homeless
Several hundred Merchant Maidens
Turned to these their kindly brothers,
Begged them for accommodation,
Until Queen Street could receive them,
Till they were equipped with shelters,
And their gentle brothers heard them,
Chivalrous, could not refuse them.

Farewell to Stewart's

It was obvious, however, to the Board and to the Staff of the two Schools that the system operating at Stewart's was impossible and that alterative arrangements would have to be made. In March 1940 parents were circulated about their reactions to a mass School evacuation; at meetings generally unfavourable views were expressed but lengthy discussions took place during the summer on the serious possibility of evacuating the Ladies' College as a unit to St.Andrews, sharing accommodation with St.Leonard's, while George Watson's Ladies' College was to go north to Elgin. The plans fell through, largely because parents felt that St.Andrews was at risk from air attack and Elgin was too remote, and a second evacuation scheme to Galashiels was also a non-starter. Any parents who felt strongly about it had evacuated their children at the very beginning of the war; the others wanted to keep them at home, whatever the risks. Under strong pressure from the Education Board, the Scottish Education Department agreed to allow the Senior School to return to Queen Street on November 11th, 1940, where they were greeted by a reception committee of the Master, Treasurer, Secretary and their Vice-Convener; the Juniors remained for the time being at Daniel Stewart's and the Elementary at Ravelston Park.

A sixth former, new to the School on the first day back in Queen Street, wrote:

> I found myself in a brick-walled box-like place that was to be our cloakroom shelter. There was a great babble of conversation; members of staff were hurrying round seeing that everyone had a label. We went along light corridors and dark corridors, along wide corridors and narrow ones, down little flights of stairs and up big ones; I asked someone where the Latin class was; 'Old School' was the cryptic answer. Our formroom was in a delightful muddle; I was told it used to be a laundry and is now a lab. I was swept along more corridors to buy dinner tickets, then was rushed up to a mysterious room called the 'Rec.' Then came dinner; I started violently when the gong went for Grace, though I had been told what to expect. My general impressions were of long corridors, hundreds of stairs and of the contrast between the 'Old School' and the new.[7]

The girls and the Staff settled thankfully back into familiar surroundings; they were still cramped, owing to shelters in the basement and a First Aid Post in the Exam Hall, but they were home:

> There were the same comfortable Ref., the same Monday soup for dinner and the same atmosphere of friendliness and of a kind of unity which was somehow lacking in Stewart's. After a few days it scarcely seemed that we had been away.[8]

Marjorie Chaplyn commented:

> We Merchant Maidens were neither resentful nor impatient when we left Queen Street for the 'cloud-capped towers' of Daniel Stewart's College and we made the most of our sojourn at D.S.C. It has been an experience for us all and it has been salutary in that it has shown us just how strong tradition can be. It has been put to the test and I think

we are entitled to say that it has not failed.[9]

The girls threw themselves with enthusiasm into the war effort. As transport became more difficult many were cycling to school, which was now opening at 9.30 during the winter months because of black-out regulations. The Board announced that 'girls need not come into school until the second period if they are disturbed by air-raids at any time after 2 a.m.' but the night skies over Edinburgh were undisturbed. The usual knitting of blankets and comforts for the Forces went on throughout the war, and a special interest was taken in Daniel Stewart's adopted ship, the *Bencruachan*:

> On behalf of the Chinese crew the no. 1 Fireman expressed himself as follows — 'Please talkee your fliends all Chinaman velly happy for nice pleasants'. It would have done your hearts good to see the grins of delight on their yellow faces when they saw the sweets, cigarettes and woollen comforts. To the Tiny Tots who supplied the much-needed book-marks and writing materials and to all of you at College we send our best wishes and greetings.[10]

A War Savings Scheme was introduced and was so popular that by 1944 almost every girl in the School was contributing to the £3000 being collected annually. Senior girls worked in the holidays in the Post Office, the Land Army or the Forestry Commission and younger ones went berry picking in Angus, eighty girls and twenty staff in two shifts. Magazines, toys, tinfoil and sweets (now rationed) were collected for various good causes, beds maintained in the Elsie Inglis Hospital, First Aid lectures given and a GTC group formed. But many of the staff must have found day-time teaching a strain after night-time fire-watching which went on in the building every night and throughout the weekends. Two men were hired as watchers at £3 weekly, relieved on one night by the janitors or male staff and covering the neighbouring Kintore Rooms as well as the School; but women staff covered the weekends, sleeping four at a time on camp beds in the huge, dark building. The Board refused to pay them the standard 1/6 nightly food allowance, though on Sundays they could have a breakfast of 'tea, biscuits and unrationed food' if they cooked it themselves. At Ravelston Park the Matron and her husband got a flat with free coal and light and £20 in exchange for fire-watching the building.

In 1944 Marjorie Chaplyn wrote:

> Against a background of epoch-making events we continue to pursue the path of normal school activities with sundry excursions into the wider world.[11]

Bomb-shattered Caen was sent aid and the Sikorski Memorial Hospital in Warsaw benefited from an exhibition of Polish photography and costumes in the School Hall. 1944 was an eventful year: not only did the School watch the Princess Royal review the local GTC companies in Queen Street Gardens, but their name was changed in celebration of their 250th anniversary to that of their founder and they were now to be known as 'The Mary

The 250th Anniversary inspection by the Princess Royal

Erskine School' with the sub-title 'The Merchant Maiden Hospital founded in 1694 by the Company of Merchants of the City of Edinburgh and Mary Erskine'. The Anniversary service in June in St.Giles was attended by the Princess Royal and many civic and public figures, followed by a reception in the City Chambers; Edinburgh was proud to honour one of its oldest schools.

A year later, with the European war at an end and commemorated by a Victory Service at St.Giles, Marjorie Chaplyn spoke at prize-giving:

With thankfulness the end of the war found us in possession of our building, old and inadequate though it be, but regretful at discontinuing temporarily the Nursery class and bringing the two junior Prep. classes back into cramped and unsuitable accommodation in an over-crowded building.[12]

121

Juniors

She would only have to struggle for one more term with all the problems of post-war short-ages and restrictions in an ageing building. In the autumnn of 1945 she accepted a post in the English Inspectorate and went south to what can only have been a less demanding career. She had been Head through eight dramatic and exhausting years when her own aca-demic interests had been subordinated to the demands of administration and she had carried out her task nobly. The affection in which her staff and pupils held her was expressed in many ways, one of the most spontaneous tributes coming from a Second Year pupil:

Farewell, dear Headmistress,
You are going afar,
But we will never forget you
Wherever you are.
Good-bye Dr.Chaplyn,
We know you will often see
In happy reveries
The girls of the M.E.S.G.
The School won't forget you
Our hearts will remain true,
And you'll always remember
The girls in red and blue.

REFERENCES

1, 2	INSPECTORS' REPORT, 1938.
3	E.B.M., OCTOBER, 1938.
4, 5	M.M., 1939.
6, 7, 8, 9	M.M., 1940.
10	M.M., 1941.
11	PRINCIPAL'S REPORT, 1944.
12	PRINCIPAL'S REPORT, 1945.

Muriel Jennings

CHAPTER 7

1946 - 1966

*'No-one can complain that
school life is dull'*

The Education Board broke new ground in the summer of 1945 in appointing Marjorie Chaplyn's successor; for the first time in its history the School had a Head who was not a Scot. Of the fifteen applicants for the post, ten were from England; four, like Muriel Jennings, were Heads of other schools. Educated at St.Paul's School and holding degrees in History from both Oxford and Cambridge, Muriel Jennings had been for eleven years Headmistress of Pate's Grammar School for Girls, an old and independent foundation, now threatened with absorption into the State system. At Cheltenham she had taken considerable interest in local affairs and was also nationally involved in the work of the Y.M.C.A. and the National Council of Women. She was frank in her reasons for looking for a new post: she had no wish to remain at Pate's under the new system promised by the Labour government and saw the Mary Erskine School as one whose endowed status seemed secure. She was in her early forties when she took up her post in January, 1946. Tall, with a commanding presence, elegantly dressed and with a distinctly English intonation, her new pupils found her very different from the traditional Scots image of a woman teacher. She recalled an early incident:

> When I arrived at Queen Street the War was barely over. Dr.Chaplyn had been a splendid Headmistress under difficult circumstances and had made many innovations, including the change of name. I inherited all the benefits of her work with the accompanying difficulties smoothed away. The basement cloakrooms were shored up into narrow passages and one morning the electricity failed about 8.50 a.m. and visions of the London Tube disaster rose before me. I was down those two flights of stairs and into the melée in a matter of seconds. How grateful I was for my English voice. 'It's Miss Jennings' went round, and in silence form by form filed up into its own room, some shoeless, some hatted.[1]

The tone is as unmistakable as the 'English accent'; a firm disciplinarian with considerable distaste for a 'melée' or for any failure in self-control either in an individual or in a

The Staff

crowd, she expected her pupils to reflect her own image of a professional woman in what was still very much a man's world. To her girls, staff and parents she was autocracy personified. Bred in the old tradition where a Headmistress's word was law, she would tolerate neither criticism nor opposition, and legends about her high-handedness circulated in Edinburgh, often gaining in the retelling. Girls could be reduced to tears for failing to make the correct curtsey at a Prize-giving rehearsal, staff bluntly informed that their style of dress was unsuitable and parents summoned to her study to be told exactly what University the Head had decided their daughter should proceed to. Not surprisingly, methods of self-protection were developed: girls maintained a demure front and expressed their feelings in graffiti in the attics of the Old Building. Staff united in total solidarity to protect whoever of their number was currently under attack and parents learned that to send a father alone to discuss his daughter's problems often proved the best method of persuasion. In fairness to the Head it must be admitted that she was fully aware that the School was housed in an extremely dangerous building and that a tradition of firm discipline was essential in case an emergency arose. She also misunderstood the Scots temperament and made the mistake of thinking that reticence expressed agreement and acceptance; faced with firm and informed opposition, she would respect her opponent's point and would capitulate with considerable charm and grace.

She was to find that her relationship with her employers at Merchants' Hall was less easy than the one she had enjoyed with the Governors at Pate's. It was hard to accept the fact that the Board saw her as an employee who was expected to toe the line which they laid down on Schools' policy. She frankly admitted that she found charm a useful means of getting her way, using social contacts outside School to make allies and 'spending a fortune on evening frocks'. She enjoyed social life but found Edinburgh society provincial and male-dominated, a difficult situation at that period for a successful professional woman. Her strongest allies were the School's successive Vice-Conveners who acted as plenipotentiaries between her and the Education Board. With them she generally enjoyed a very happy relationship; it was unfortunate that a constant state of running warfare existed between her and the Company's Secretary during her time as Head and, although as a 'bonny fechter' she rather enjoyed the situation, she admitted frankly that she was never good at fighting men on their own ground and found it all rather tiring.

By her English standards the School was deficient in many ways. It needed a strong VIth Form and a good Prefect system; she also felt, perhaps wrongly, that the girls were too lesson-bound and showed little interest in activities outside the classroom. She felt that they had a limited cultural background and had very little knowledge of the wider world even in Edinburgh. Her first Report after two terms in office was withering:

> The Senior School presents the problems that exist among adolescents in many places. The girls are lacking in community spirit and very few attend meetings or societies. It will be my definite aim to try to give many outside interests and to make the girls feel that there are always worth-while things to be done in the School building apart from lessons. At present the cinema is presenting to a large portion their ideal of life.[2]

This kind of sweeping statement from a new Head was not likely to be popular with Edinburgh parents. Five years of wartime conditions with winter black-out and limited transport had kept children housebound, especially those who lived outwith the City, and there was some resentment that an incomer was criticising the Edinburgh system. However, with energy and determination Muriel Jennings set about putting her stamp on the School, initiating a series of changes at a speed often disconcerting both to girls and staff.

Always in favour of single-school education, she saw to it that the Preparatory Department was re-established in the Queen Street building and the Nursery class revived, feeling that the presence of tiny children could do nothing but good in a community of women. She re-arranged the classroom structure by giving each class its own form-room where all except practical lessons were taught; this saved a great deal of movement about an inconvenient and structurally unsound building and released several rooms for use by the returning Primary and Nursery departments. Heads of Department, jealous of their traditional status, were allotted minute study rooms in 'Spinsters' Alley', the old piano practice rooms, and she herself took over the former Guild Room as an office. With nine hundred and fifty-eight girls on the roll, the building was grossly overcrowded and there was great pressure on the dining and recreation Halls; a staggered lunchbreak with two sittings helped to ease some of the congestion and order was assured by putting prefects in charge of tables with instructions to maintain order and promote conversation. With most pupils leaving after Vth year there were only eleven girls in the VIth Form and, with servicemen returning to higher education, there was considerable competition for University places, preference being given to VIth Form applicants. The Head set out to build up the VIth, introducing O and A Level courses alongside the Highers and seeing a dramatic rise in the numbers staying for an extra year. By the early 1960s there were over seventy girls in the VIth, usually about twenty taking University entrance a year after the more normal Scottish

In the prep.

The Prefects

Vth year. Edinburgh and St. Andrews were the first popular choices, but as the new Scottish and English Universities became available students became adventurous, lured by new courses and the joys of campus life. With her admiration for the English education system the Head encouraged Oxbridge candidates and even entered 'thirteen academically weak children' for the Oxford School Certificate in 1949, but although this was quite successful, pressure from parents and staff made it a one-off experiment.

She believed strongly in providing a varied syllabus for pupils of all abilities. By 1947 she was reporting:

> I feel we should try to be less rigid in our syllabuses and give the A classes more and varied mental food and the C classes a completely different approach. We should start from the known, the practical, the every-day angle and not expect too much in the way of written work.[3]

Science students

The Art Department

Streamed in the traditional manner, the A classes, although by the 1960s initialised from their Form mistresses' names, still regarded themselves as the School's intellectual aristocrats and were generally taught by senior and promoted Staff, while the Cs, although often considerably gifted, carried a permanent sense of inferiority and were not slow to express it:

> When we have lessons with Miss X [a Head of Department] she's so clever that we don't understand what she's saying, but [to a lesser Staff member] you're like us, you're not clever and we can understand you quite well.[4]

Muriel Jennings was well aware of this and provided, as far as was possible in an old building, at least adequate facilities in practical subjects; the result was a steady flow of girls into careers such as nursing, catering, physiotherapy, occupational therapy, pharmacy, chiropody and speech training. Art Colleges drew plenty of applicants and P.E. training, with the inspiration of a dynamic Head of Department, became a popular career choice.

The Head's policy of extending the girls' social and cultural horizons benefited everyone. Visiting lecturers to the School, outings to plays and concerts and expeditions to explore various aspects of Edinburgh life became an accepted part of the terms' programme. The School branch of the Edinburgh Schools' Citizenship Association (ESCA) flourished in the post-war climate; so did the Scripture Union, founded before the War, and junior membership of the English Speaking Union which gave opportunities to visit the United States, while one of the founders of the popular Edinburgh Schools' Scientific Society was a Queen Street girl. Travel outide Edinburgh was now taken for granted, to the potato-lifting and berry-picking camps which continued until the 1950s, the Guide and Scripture Union camps in Scotland, ski-ing in Switzerland from 1948, visits to Austria and Italy with ESCA and, most importantly, annual exchange visits to the Lycée Victor Duruy in Paris which would become an established ritual and the source of many horror stories about French school and family life. The Head was delighted to see the girls' horizons expanding but worried that the post-war generation with all these new delights had too little interest in reading apart from fiction. She did everything possible to encourage an interest in books, building up good stocks of both fiction and non-fiction material, refurnishing the Library with comfortable chairs and a good supply of periodicals and making it available for younger pupils, but as in so many other fields she was hampered by lack of space in a cramped building.

Games continued to be played at Inverleith, and dancing and gym somehow carried on under appalling conditions at Queen Street. Sport, which had gone through difficult times in the War, flourished from the '50s with frequent triumphs and awards. The traditional

Home Economics

Usher Hall Prizegiving

hockey, tennis and some netball were the options available and swimming continued at Drumsheugh or George Watson's Baths.

Both Drama and Music were enthusiastically supported, although also affected by the lack of facilities. With the introduction of good stage-lighting more ambitious plays could be presented, and the '50s and '60s saw major productions of Shakespeare, Molière, Sheridan, Wilde and Shaw as well as minor efforts by the Juniors. The Orchestra, disbanded during the War years, was revived in 1950, initially with sixteen string players; six years later it had grown to a strong forty-nine players and the School's formal occasions were musically supported by them and by enthusiastic Senior and Junior choirs. The singers had several opportunities to perform publicly in the '40s and '50s when state occasions brought Royalty to Edinburgh. In 1949, when Princess Elizabeth and the Duke of Edinburgh were installed as honorary members of the Merchant Company, girls from George Watson's and Mary Erskine sang for them, while at the Coronation visit in 1953 they joined massed school choirs to sing at Murrayfield. The Head took great pleasure in seeing her well turned-out girls at state occasions; always an elegant dresser, she liked to see the whole school on parade in summer dresses 'like a lot of sweet peas', while the Duke of Edinburgh's praise of the prefects' summer dresses which she had designed, worn in 1955 when they lunched at Merchants' Hall, was a source of great pride. On such occasions the girls were briefed on the correct protocol for meeting royalty, rehearsed in curtseys and sent out immaculate, even wearing long white gloves. Protocol was also observed for the VIth Form dances, introduced in 1956. Formal dress was *de rigeur* and partners' names and those of the schools which they attended had to be submitted by parents. Another uniform change was seen in 1952 after the Education Board had observed with some concern that

> A Corporation School had recently adopted a uniform similar to that worn by the Mary Erskine School with the same tie and scarf. It was suggested that a new tie and scarf should be introduced with the stripes of different widths and that the shield of the Merchant Company coat of arms in full colour should be the School badge on the blazer and beret and also on the tie; the letters M.E.S.G. should appear on the blazer pocket below the shield.[5]

This was followed by the registering of the School's own coat of arms as a cadet of the Merchant Company whose arms were displayed on a lozenge, heraldically correct for females, while the traditional motto *Mitis et Fortis* was now officially adopted.

By the 1950s the condition of the Queen Street building was a source of considerable anxiety to the Education Board and to everyone who worked in it. No major repairs or reconstruction had been carried out since Mary Clarke's time over forty years earlier, and occasional redecoration had never addressed the main problem of structural safety. In 1950 Mr. Wilson, the official Schools' architect and Clerk of Works, presented an alarming report to the Board in which no punches were pulled:

Installation of the Merchant Company Arms at Roxburgh Kirk, 1955

This would appear to be an opportunity to review the position regarding the Mary Erskine School for Girls when long term policy as affecting development, extension or rehousing of schools generally is being considered. When in 1938 I became actively interested in the maintenance of the school, the instruction was received from the then Superintendent of Works to take no liberties with the old building structurally as the fabric could not be trusted and that no major expenditure could be envisaged there as the Old Building (the west wing) had a doubtful life in its present form.

The northern portion of the Old Building has been elaborately shored up and stiffened by cast iron columns and steel beams. The date of their introduction is not known, yet in spite of these props settlement and weakening are observed today. When air-raid shelters were built in 1940 in the basement of the Old Building it was discovered that there was no foundation to the south wall of the Hall and this was then partly under-pinned. Several flaws in plaster-work on walls and ceilings have revealed the most jerry construction and indicated movement of the building while settlement in floors has been noted. Sufficient dangerous plaster-work has already been dealt with to influence me to express apprehension as to the advisability of accommodating pupils in this building.

The Roof Garden

While undertaking painter-work in the Staff dining-room during the vacation the painter drew attention to the swinging ceiling; the plasterer immediately investigated this and little or no encouragement was required to bring down approximately two tons of plaster, some three inches thick in place of the standard three-quarters. It should be noted that this ceiling appeared sound, having no cracks or bulges.

In view of these disclosures, can any of the ceilings now passed as safe be counted on for one year ahead? The writer would be glad to show any deputation over the school and point out defects of which the Board understandably have no knowledge. In short I would welcome any steps being taken to impress on those concerned the necessity for giving highest priority to the question of forming a definite policy for the future of the Mary Erskine School for Girls.[6]

The Board noted the report and some repairs to the most obviously dangerous ceilings were carried out, along with the redecoration of the Hall. This pleased everyone, though less happy was the decision to remove the original Dux Prize-winner boards dating from the 1870s and to replace them with a Prize-winners' book.

But the old building could not be placated with superficial plaster and paint. It bided its time until January 20th, 1956 when the Janitor phoned the Head to report that thirteen of the Junior School ceilings had collapsed during the night. Muriel Jennings went over at once and recalled that 'she didn't like the feel of the building.' In the afternoon she went back, accompanied by the Secretary and Vice-Convener, and it was agreed that this part of the building was unusable and that accommodation was urgently needed for the Juniors. Characteristically Muriel Jennings knew exactly how to handle the situation; the house opposite her flat in Ainslie Place was for sale and she ordered the Board to offer for it immediately. Nothing was said to the parents until the Monday morning when the girls came in to school. The Juniors were addressed by the Head and told that they were to stay at home for three days, that 'alterations had to be made to the building' and that in no circumstances was any parent to write or telephone to the School during that time. It is a tribute to her reputation with Mary Erskine parents that she was obeyed and that, by the time the children returned, 18 Ainslie Place had been got ready for them after three days of frantic activity.

An emergency of this kind was meat and drink to the Head. Apparently tireless herself, she expected nothing less than total commitment from her staff and would drive them to the limit, though never losing her understanding of normal human weakness. 'You must understand that people get very tired', she often said and never failed to express appreciation for anyone who had worked hard for her and for the School. Timetables were as far as possible arranged to ease a heavy teaching day and Queen Street staff recall with gratitude the bonus of a fixed short afternoon once a week which it was hoped would help to recharge their batteries. The 1956 crisis called on everyone, staff and girls alike:

No-one can complain that our school life is dull. Scarcely had we recovered from the excitements of the first term when the walls and ceilings of the Junior School began to collapse all at once and a large part of the building had to be evacuated. One third of the school is now sealed off behind cardboard partitions behind which workmen are busy tearing down the whole interior of the building. This sudden disintegration surprised no-one; indeed it is astonishing that the building lasted as long as it did. While the harassed Higher candidates were furiously trying to acquire some knowledge, the so-called 'leisure class' (the VI Form) was tying pieces of coloured string on every chair in sight and then carrying all the furniture in the building up and down several flights of stairs and even along Queen Street. This aroused considerable interest in Edinburgh. It was very good for the VI Form, even if the furniture did not benefit from the treatment.[7]

The Board expressed its thanks to 'Miss Jennings, her deputy and the Staff for the manner in which they kept the School running' and voted £15 and a letter of appreciation to the Janitor. By May they had approved plans for making part of the Queen Street building safe but, hoping to be able to purchase the property adjoining 18 Ainslie Place, delayed a decision on the rest of the building; in the end it was agreed to demolish the Art Room, placing a flat roof over the third floor and creating a new Biology Room, the whole process to take about six months. In June Muriel Jennings looked back over five months and reported:

THE SHORT INTERVAL M. ANDERSON

Short Interval

THE LONG INTERVAL

M. ANDERSON

16

Long Interval

The mess from fallen plaster made the whole school dirty and nine of the twelve cleaners refused to work and left. I have been fortunate in getting quite a different type of woman. The Janitor behaved splendidly but got very tired. At the beginning of February the coal supply, as usual, gave out; the boiler-man decided he was overworked and gave a week's notice. After losing about a third of the building I put three Preparatory forms in the Kintore Rooms. They are near and have a hall for dancing and play but, as they are let for functions, senior girls must go in at least twice a week at midday and early next morning to remove and replace desks and chairs. The first two Junior classes I sent to Simpson House. Again furniture had to be shifted every day but not far and the children were able to manage for themselves. Two forms had to live in corridors in the main building, so do the Catering Superintendent's stores as her room is considered unsafe. The loss of the kitchen staff's cloakrooms, one staffroom and one staff cloakroom made things very uncomfortable but morale remained high. Except for denying the use of the School to outside bodies the School activities have not been curtailed in any way. I cannot speak too highly of the loyalty and adaptability of the teaching staff and the Janitor.[8]

137

THE CHARGE OF THE DINNER QUEUE

(WITH APOLOGIES TO TENNYSON)

Half an inch, half an inch,
Half an inch onward,
Into the Dining Room
Crept the four hundred.
" Forward the Dinner Queue!
Charge for the Hatch," they cried :
Into the Dining Room
Surged the four hundred.

" Forward, the Dinner Queue ! "
Was there a girl who lagged ?
Not tho' they all knew
Some one had blunder'd :
Failed had the bell to ring
Late was their Dinner Time
Theirs not to reason why,
Theirs but to do or die :
Into the Dining Room
Pressed the four hundred.

Pres. to the right of them,
Staff to the left of them,
Cooks in front of them,
All shouting out orders;
Stormed at with shrieks and threats,
Boldly they surged right on,
Unto their mince and spud,
Unto their steamed spice pud.
Dauntless four hundred !

When can their glory fade ?
O the wild charge they made !
All the world wondered.
Honour the charge they made !
Honour these Merchant Maids,
    Noble four hundred !

MARGARET T. WILLIAMSON, VA.
14

The Charge of the Dinner Queue

It was always believed by the Queen Street girls that the middle 'M' in their Head's name stood for 'Mafeking'; the Year of the Collapse certainly showed in her all the spirit that won the Empire. By the following year the editors of the 'Merchant Maiden' could report:

After months of obscure bangings behind mysterious partitions the reconstructed part of the School like the phoenix has risen from the ashes or rather the rubble and was suddenly revealed to us the other morning in all its new-painted splendour. The colour scheme in the corridors is a delicate turquoise and white with 'what-daring-yellow' doors.[9]

The Head, always good in relations with workmen, praised the builders, painters and joiners for their co-operation and thanked providence for a mild winter. After five disorganised terms she and her staff were exhausted but they had weathered the crisis, and the establishment of the Preparatory in Ainslie Place made Queen Street overcrowding a little more bearable. But it was apparent to everyone connected with the School that the Board could delay no longer: Mary Erskine must be rebuilt on a new site.

The relocation of Queen Street was not a new scheme; it had been under discussion since the beginning of the century when there had been talk of rebuilding on the James Gillespie's site. The erection of the New Wing had shelved the problem; but the failure to rebuild the westward section and forty years of piecing and patching had put too much strain on buildings never designed to withstand the pressures of heavy traffic on both sides of their walls. The Board had always known they must rebuild; back in 1936 Sir William Keith in a Founders' Day speech had pointed out:

A public body meanly housed is a body meanly regarded. Was it too much to hope that a second Mary Erskine might arise who would obtain a site and a building for the premier girls' school in Scotland more worthy of her fame?[10]

The crisis twenty years later precipitated action. The Board immediately approached the Scottish Education Department 'for help in acquiring a site for building a new school in place of the present Queen Street'. They already had the ideal site in mind.

The old Ravelston Estate lay to the west of Edinburgh in the district known as Ravelston Dykes. Largely rural until the 1930s, it was now surrounded by quality villas whose owners were likely to favour private education for their young. Another Company boys' School, Daniel Stewart's College, was in the neighbourhood and a private School, St.George's, provided excellent facilities for girls, but a good local bus service meant that Ravelston was within easy reach of central Edinburgh and the Mary Erskine School's wide catchment area. The estate had been laid out in the seventeenth century by the Foulis family whose most distinguished figure, Sir John, was a contemporary of Mary Erskine. It had later passed to the Keith family who had replaced the Foulis tower-house with a handsome mansion, set above the original seventeenth-century garden. Sir Walter Scott, a friend and visitor, is said to have based the garden lay-out of the mansion of Tullyveolan in *Waverley* on the parterres of Ravelston; another contemporary 'literary' visitor to the house was the precocious 'Pet Marjory' Fleming. By descent from the Keiths the estate came to the Murray family and thence to Mrs.Clark who was the owner in the early 1950s.

The ninety-acre site was already zoned by the local authority to accommodate a school, housing and open green space. For the Board it was the ideal property: facing south across gently rolling fields, backed with woodland, the old house could provide a visual punctuation point to contemporary buildings and was spacious enough to offer elegant rooms for formal occasions as well as ample teaching space and a flat for a Headmistress. The sunny parkland would be ideal for tennis courts and hockey pitches, and in these open spaces children could enjoy fresh air and exercise in perfect safety. Five years earlier the Board had begun discussions with Mrs.Clark's agents but these had come to nothing; the owner wanted to leave the house to the Church of Scotland for use as an Eventide Home and the grounds to Edinburgh Corporation as a public park, but as the Board discovered in July:

> The proprietrix was a lady of almost ninety and her Law Agents had been unable to get definite instructions from her. The matter had been taken up with the S.E.D. and the Town Council and the Town Clerk had now intimated that the Planning Sub-Committee would be prepared, on submission of a formal application and sufficiently detailed plans, to grant consent to the proposed development of the site.[11]

The Ravelston estate was surveyed in the autumn of 1956; it was not until January 1960 that any further progress took place, though the Board set up a Building Committee for its two girls' schools in 1958, looking at others recently built and discussing possible architects. Meanwhile Queen Street had shown further signs of deterioration in the autumn of 1957, causing two terms of disruption involving the loss of the Cookery Room and the Staff Room and the daily carrying of lunches to the Juniors in the Kintore Rooms. 'Remedial steps in the region of £15,000 to £20,00' were seen by the Board as 'regrettable but unavoidable, as they could not take any risk where the safety of the children was concerned'. Early in 1960 Mrs.Clark's agents wrote to the Board, asking how much land they wished to purchase and enquiring if they would also be interested in the mansion and in its outlying offices. A price of at least £125,000 was suggested for the land to include £17,000 for the house, its walled garden and the extensive out-buildings. It was hinted that the Board would be wise to buy all the land zoned for school use 'to prevent a speculative builder moving in and to give over a period of years surplus ground which might yield a substantial profit'.

Bearing in mind that the extensive grounds of Ravelston could also provide playing fields for Daniel Stewart's College and that the two Schools' playing fields at Inverleith could therefore be sold, the Board decided to offer £125,000 for the whole estate, arguing that the agents might accept a low offer to avoid excessive death duties. They miscalculated; a much higher offer had been made by one of the Company's members, Mr.Thomas Boland, and had been accepted.

All was not lost: Mr.Boland's building interests meant that he was anxious to develop the western side of the site but was prepared to sell to the Board the mansion with its access drives and the grounds with the exception of the walled garden and the outbuildings. In June 1960 the land and the mansion were purchased for £110,700; since the portion retained by Mr.Boland would have been of little use to the School, the Board could congratulate themselves on a small saving. An architect, Thomas Kinninmonth, had already been appointed and was preparing plans; with the appointment of engineers and quantity surveyors, it seemed as if the building of the new School was under way.

Time passed; plans were presented, rejected, re-presented, rejected again; Building Committees formed and re-formed; accounts were endlessly discussed as costs inevitably rose with the passing of time. The architect estimated the final cost of the school would be in the region of one and three quarter million pounds; too much, said the Board. The standards of materials and finishes advocated by Mr.Kinninmonth were too high, 75% above those in recent Local Authority School building; economies must be made. In the autumn of 1962 yet another revised draft plan was drawn up at a more realistic cost and accepted. The architect estimated a further seven months would be needed to prepare the detailed plans and suggested that tenders might be sought in a year's time. In the interval extensive and expensive dry-rot eradication was carried out in Ravelston House; while this was going on lead was stripped from the roof and had to be replaced, reconditioned gas street lamps installed to light the drive were stolen, and Thomas Boland's bulldozers levelled the Foulis' fine old walled garden for the erection of executive housing. At Queen Street it seemed as if the new School was an unattainable dream; firmly warned off the site by the Head, staff and parents would sneak out at weekends to see if there was any sign of progress and return to report no change on the Ravelston front. Early in 1964 things at last began to move. The Dean of Guild approved the plans, MacLeod's tender was found acceptable by the Board and the Countess of Mar and Kellie laid the foundation stone. Building at last could begin. The contractors estimated that summer, 1966 was a realistic date for completion and that the School might expect to start that autumn session in the new building. With a firm date ahead the Board agreed in March 1965 to sell the Queen Street site to City Wall Developments for demolition.

In 1966 with building well ahead the Board paid an official visit to the site: 'all agreed that when the New School was completed it would be a very fine one and that the architecture was well suited to its surroundings'. Good use had been made of the falling ground and of the fine views in all directions. A series of linked white blocks fanned eastwards from the old mansion, most no more than two storeys high. All had large windows to frame views of grass, trees and the unparalleled Edinburgh skyline to the east. Laboratories, Art rooms, Library, gyms were all of a quality unknown at Queen Street; a fine Assembly Hall with a professionally lit stage, large dining-rooms backed by modern kitchens, tennis courts, hockey pitches and a superb swimming pool would, all were confident, be ready by June. A relaxed flitting from Queen Street could take place during the summer holidays and the girls could start the autumn session in their new building.

Hopes died as the summer passed and the building was still not completed. Muriel Jennings had already announced her decision to retire in December 1966, planning to oversee the move and the first term in the new building before the arrival of her successor. These plans had to be modified. Jean Thow was appointed as the incoming Head in June on the understanding that she would take up office in January 1967; but the move from Queen Street to Ravelston was not to take place until October 1966, in the middle of the autumn term.

Dancing class

When the 'Merchant Maiden' went to press in the early summer of 1966 the Editors were still sanguine:

So the Big Change foretold for so long is to come about at last. When the doors close behind us at the end of this session it will be for the last time. During the summer holidays something resembling a new Great Trek will be taking place westwards towards Ravelston. Next term Queen Street will seem unusually quiet — there will be no crowds of returning pupils surging round the school door. It will all be happening a few miles up the road. Ravelston will have become the new home of the Mary Erskine School for Girls. As sixth-formers with long experience of life at Queen Street we cannot help wondering rather uneasily about the effect of new surroundings on the Mary Erskine girl. The distant sound of a cuckoo (or even of a wood-pigeon) can hardly give the same intellectual stimulus as the roar of traffic on Queen Street and the unloading of milk crates in the lane. We fear that easy living at Ravelston may produce poorer physical specimens in the years to come. There will no longer be four flights of stairs to scale in double-quick time. And what modern central-heating system can produce the rapid changes in temperature which have for decades kept us so mentally alert?[12]

The Great Trek of October 1966 was masterminded by the Head and, typically, proceeded with apparent smoothness and efficiency. The Juniors were sent ahead to be set-tled on the new site; the Seniors enjoyed a brief holiday while a fleet of pantechnicons transported the entire contents of the Queen Street buildings up the Dykes to Ravelston. Staff had toiled for days packing books, stationery, files, lab. equipment, pictures, plants and the assorted detritus of long residence. Huge and heavy Victorian bookcases and desks were lodged incongruously in light modern rooms; there was at the same time somehow too much space and not nearly enough. Dazed with exhaustion, the Staff who endured the move can remember little of it except the sense of triumph when it was all over. On October 24th the first official Assembly was held in the new Hall when the guest speak-er, Mary Clarke, drew together the threads of the old life and the new experiences awaiting the first Ravelston generation and spoke of 'the noble buildings and grounds which the Company in its age-long tradition of generosity has fashioned as a new home for its oldest school'. A new phase in the Family's history had begun.

Dogged traditionalists, many of the girls found it hard to adjust to new travel patterns and unfamiliar surroundings; there was so much light and space, almost too much out-doors. They huddled together in classrooms in the lunch interval; driven out by Staff determined that they should enjoy their new amenities, they crept back to the protection of desks and blackboards. The younger ones responded joyfully:

Our old school has just been dimolished. It is being made into offissis. It is just as well becos its walls were cracked and the roof was coming to bits. It was so noisy with cars and lorries that I had to block my ear drums. Here it is lovely and qiet and we can see the green leeves. Our new school is much nicer, frinstance the jims are super and they have lots of apparatis. I have so much space to run about in that when I have run right round the jim I'm quite puffed out. We have a playground so big that you don't youshally bump into anyone. Yes certainly our new school is better than the old one.[13]

But the seniors were not all so enthusiastic:

All the modern equipment and facilities at Ravelston hold no fascination for some of us. I am referring to those new contraptions and apparatus in the gyms — ideal for games-mad enthusiasts but to more inferior gymnasts such as myself sheer torture. How often have I longed for those dark shadowy corners in the little gyms at Queen Street where we were so crammed that there was no room to indulge in the fantastic head-stands and spectacular leaps that we do here. I dislike the size of the windows in the gyms and swimming pool. I think I know how a gold-fish in a tank feels and if anyone is unfortunate enough to have a gym lesson when the juniors are at their interval then my complaints will be understood. They stare, plainly fascinated. Does one continue one's efforts and pretend they aren't there or stare back coldly with all the dignity of superior years?[14]

Muriel Jennings remained in office until the end of the autumn term; she was determined as far as possible to have everything up and running so that her successor could settle in with

Corridors of cracked mosaic,
Peeling paintwork.
Workmen drilling in the street,
Traffic, noise.
Desks with splinters,
Cloakrooms dimly lit,
Coal-dust.
The rec. room, and the gangway, and
Don't sit on the counter, and
Don't eat on the roof-garden, and
Enter by the Teak Door.
Scaffolding through shattered glass.
Jagged, naked shell.
Dirt and rubble.
Desolation.
Desecration. . . .

Bright, white squares.
Clear, clean, blue sky.
Walls of glass, sunshine,
Light pouring in.
Picture windows, picture postcard view.
Mediterranean warmth, turquoise, gently lapping.
Soft languorous music.
Icy, freezing wind-tunnel blowing wet air.
Sudden rainstorm sweeping over,

Goodbye to Queen Street

the minimum of stress. She was happy with the new building; some areas still awaited completion but the general effect was all that could be wished. New and old combined happily. The girls could be reminded of the School's history in the Crush Hall which displayed the table carpet from the Merchant Maiden Hospital, Mary Clarke's kneeling Maiden, the original of Mary Tweedie's Tree of the School's History and the Guild's gift of glass doors engraved by Mrs.Turner with portraits of Merchants and former Heads, views of earlier School buildings, sprays of broom and Marjorie Chaplyn's favourite quotation:

New Days. New Ways. Pass By. Love Stays.

Many tributes were paid to Muriel Jennings on her retirement. After twenty-one years as Head she had become an Edinburgh institution and the source of many good stories. Tireless herself, she had always expected total effort and commitment from staff and girls alike; in this she followed the traditions already laid down by earlier Heads. She loved her girls, from the seniors whose careers were firmly directed on the right paths and followed with real interest down to the tiny children in the Nursery who had an annual ritual of marking her birthday with the presentation of a posy tied with the School colours. She was proud that her lasting memorial would be the New School to whose planning she had devoted so many hours of her busy life; she was happy too that her retirement home was close enough to the railway to ensure ease of return to the city where her memory would certainly not be forgotten.

Her chapter can end fittingly with a story of the last hours in Queen Street. At the end of the final school day the Head went down to the cloakrooms to make sure that the girls had cleared out all their property. She expected to find them deserted, but they were in fact full of activity. Armed with screwdrivers and pliers, the Merchant Maidens were collecting souvenirs of the old building — door handles, lavatory chains and (to the Head's horror) switch-plates from the lethal electric light system. Retribution was swift. The staff, enjoying a farewell formal tea upstairs, were deployed to their respective classrooms where the pupils were lined up and frisked for the souvenirs concealed in schoolbags and about their persons and which formed sizeable piles of nineteenth-century hardware. When the last culprit had disgorged her property the Head dismissed the School. It is worthy of record that no punishments were imposed on the girls: it was the staff who did without their tea.

REFERENCES

1	MURIEL JENNINGS, LETTER TO AUTHOR, 1992.
2	PRINCIPAL'S REPORT, 1946.
3	PRINCIPAL'S REPORT, 1947.
4	SAID TO THE AUTHOR!
5	E.B.M. MARCH, 1952.
6	REPORT TO E.B., MAY, 1950.
7	M.M., 1956.
8	PRINCIPAL'S REPORT, 1956.
9	M.M., 1957.
10	FOUNDERS' DAY SPEECH, 1936.
11	E.B.M., JULY, 1956.
12	M.M., 1966.
13, 14	M.M., 1968.

Jean Thow

For Muriel Jennings' successor the Board reverted to tradition and chose a Scot. A Modern Languages graduate of St.Andrews University, Jean Thow was a considerable German scholar, widely read in literature and theology and a keen golfer whose game had been perfected on the windy courses around Carnoustie. She came to Edinburgh from an Oxford post as Headmistress of Greycotes School. At the formal dedication of the Ravelston building by the Moderator of the General Assembly of the Church of Scotland on January 10th, 1967, she was installed as Headmistress of the Mary Erskine School by the Master of the Merchant Company whose guests included the Lord Provost of the City of Edinburgh, leading figures in Scottish education, the architect of the new building and the President of the Former Pupils' Guild. In her speech the Head pledged herself to her new responsibilities:

> Already I have felt the pulse of the school in the kindness of the Master, in the generosity and industry of the Company of Merchants and its officials, in the legacy of my great predecessors, in the encouragement of the Principals of the other Merchant Schools, in the loyalty of the Former Pupils, in the goodwill of the Staff and in the presence of many friends of the school and its wider community. On occasions like this past, present and future are telescoped and time stands still. I honour the trust which the Company of Merchants of the City of Edinburgh has placed in me and enter respectfully upon the office of Headmistress. With the strength which I am given and the help of all the people here assembled I shall serve and love this school.[1]

The service was followed by a banquet lunch-party at Merchants' Hall for the guests of honour, including the School's Heads of Department and Prefects. An occasion of importance had been marked with the Merchant Company's traditional dignity and ceremony.

Twelve years later on the occasion of the Former Pupils' leaving presentation to Jean Thow on her retirement, the Guild President said that to her the Headmistress was the embodiment of the School motto – *Mitis et Fortis*. It was a shrewd comment. The Head's

Inauguration of the new Principal

gentle courtesy was as much a part of her as her complete honesty and integrity and her inbuilt belief that truth should never be hidden or fudged, however unpleasant the consequences might be. Her strong moral principles allowed nothing but the best from herself, her staff and her pupils; a scholar herself, she expected the highest standards in academic work but had great understanding and admiration for those whose skills lay in other fields. Under her administration the school's art, music and sport were to develop to a very high standard; enjoying outdoor life herself, she encouraged a wide variety of outdoor activities from sailing to hill-walking, and her love of Europe's cultural heritage gave backing to any members of staff who wanted to take girls to visit classical sites in Rome or skiing in Austria. She was an able administrator with a belief in accurate record-keeping that was often the despair of busy staff, but she kept her eye on every cog in the school's complicated machinery and knew every girl as a personality as well as from statistics on her record card. She adopted the school's traditions as if she had herself been reared a Merchant Maiden, gave continuous support to the Former Pupils' Guild, now housed in their own room in Ravelston House, and soon secured a reputation in Edinburgh and in educational circles as an excellent hostess and an informed speaker. Within the school her own temperament sometimes made her seem withdrawn, but her isolation was perhaps partly due to deafness which she bore stoically and covered with great skill.

The first generation of Ravelston girls, revelling in the spacious, light building and in the opportunities provided in laboratories, art rooms, gyms and libraries, probably had few regrets for the old School building. In the Queen Street which they had left the demolition crews moved fast to reduce the shaky structure to rubble. The Hall, where Chopin had performed in 1848 and where Cortot had played the same pieces again one hundred and one years later, disappeared with its twelve white caryatid ladies, its fine moulded ceiling and its mirrors which had reflected generations of little white-gloved girls practicing their schottisches and polkas. In its place rose a characterless office block which the developers would christen Erskine House; in 1975 the Former Pupils installed a plaque to commemorate the old school. A more lasting reminder of their past had come into their hands on the death of Margaret Sommerville who left to the Guild her manuscript History of the School from its foundation. This was published in 1970 for the Queen Street Centenary and republished in 1993 in time for the Tercentenary of the School's foundation.

Demolition at Queen Street (Photograph RCAHMS)

The School roll for the combined Primary and Secondary sections stood in the middle nine hundreds at this period. With a lively Junior School as its base, Mary Erskine's prospects looked good, while at the top end more and more girls were opting to stay on for VIth Form courses. Jean Thow encouraged this tendency, creating in 1970 a homogeneous VIth Form to replace the previous academic and practical sections and giving the girls their own attractive Common Room. A Level and Higher work was supplemented

'She Stoops to Conquer'

by Post-Higher and General Interest courses which brought in visiting speakers and took the girls out of School to visit a variety of sites. Some of these courses were shared with the VIth Form of Daniel Stewart's, as were many dramatic productions from 1969. Performances became more ambitious with the opportunities provided by large stages and a mixed cast and included *Caesar and Cleopatra*, *The Happiest Days of Your Life*, *The Caucasian Chalk Circle* and *Antigone*, performed at one or other of the Schools or at the ChurchHill Theatre. In 1972 the tradition of performing a School Musical was launched with a production of *Iolanthe*, the Juniors presented *Joseph and his Technicolour Dream Coat* two years later, and 1976 saw *The Boy Friend*. A tradition grew up of an annual VIth Form Revue as well as a Leavers' entertainment for the Staff. In 1974 this took the form of an Edwardian Croquet Match, played by Staff and VIth Form teams on the lawn of Ravelston House against a backdrop of blazing rhododendron blossom. The Prefects were seen as key figures in developing a Ravelston ethos and were given considerable responsibility. All this activity made for a busy and happy VIth Form, and in her annual Prize-giving Address the Head liked to pay tribute to her leaving girls, stressing their achievements and the service which they had given to the School. Every year the majority went on to higher education in Universities and Colleges in Scotland and England with science-related career courses becoming an increasingly popular option.

The introduction of the Promoted Posts system in 1972 gave an administrative and pastoral structure to both Senior and Junior Schools which greatly relieved Jean Thow's heavy work-load. Staff were appointed whose remit was to supervise the conduct and progress of the girls in their charge as well as to handle any personal difficulties that could affect their school life. Detailed records were kept and frequent discussion meetings enabled the Headmistress to have an overall view of the School at all levels. The development of a Careers Advice system was also valuable; visiting speakers saw the girls in groups and individually to advise on careers, an innovation welcomed by parents who valued the chance to discuss their daughters' futures with informed professionals. Opportunities were made

Croquet Match, Staff v. VI Form

The Home Economics Department

for visits to hospitals at IVth Year level to investigate career prospects in nursing-related areas and for work experience in business and industry, backed by the development of a strong Business Studies Department. The three Sciences attracted very large numbers of girls; this was not surprising, given the excellent laboratory provision and the wide range of careers at all levels which were now available for women in science-related subjects. In Ravelston House the Home Economics Department provided not only excellent facilities for Cookery but lively teaching in Dress-making and Embroidery for both Senior and Junior Schools. This Department played a key role in the School's dramatic productions when dozens of costumes were turned out by girls and staff; in 1975 it made attractive eighteenth-century costumes for the guides at the National Trust's Georgian House in Edinburgh which were modelled by some of the girls for a visit by the Queen Mother.

The Ravelston Art Rooms were light years away from the 'drawing from the cast' of Mary Clarke's day. A wide range of skills was taught besides painting and drawing; pottery, silversmithing, silk-screen printing, puppet-making and batik work were just some of the options available for girls at all levels of the School and shown to parents and the public at exhibitions in the Department or in the School Hall. The Music Department on the upper floors of Ravelston House was an integral part of the School's life. Its orchestra and choirs took part in all the School's formal occasions, performed at Assembly and gave frequent concerts both in the School and on special occasions in public at the Usher Hall. The 1970 Centenary Concert of the four Merchant Company Schools featured not only Constant Lambert's *Rio Grande* but a performance of William Mathias' *Veni Creator Spiritus*, specially commissioned for the occasion. Music was an integral part of their school life to many of the girls and a constant procession passed through the Hall of Ravelston House

Above *The Orchestra*

Left *Memorial Doors gifted by the Former Pupils' Guild*

and climbed the elegant curving stairs to the Music Department. On their way through the Hall, decorated as a gift to the School by former Vice-Conveners, they would glance at the attractive historical dolls displayed on the window-ledges. Made by Anne Carrick, they represented the Founder's relatives the Earl and Countess of Mar, a Merchant Maiden of the Hospital's early days and a gym-dressed pupil of the days when their maker had herself been a pupil at Queen Street.

With its extensive grounds Ravelston provided an ideal site for sport of all kinds, and ample facilities were planned which could be used not only by the girls but also by the boys from Daniel Stewart's, later to become Stewart's Melville. There were teething troubles in the early days at the school with an unfinished swimming-pool, waterlogged hockey pitches and poorly-laid tennis courts; but these problems were eventually resolved and, with excellent spacious gyms, the girls had a wide range of sports opportunities on the site, not only hockey, tennis and swimming but also lacrosse, volleyball, basketball, squash, badminton and athletics. The annual Sports became an important social occasion in the School's year while successes both for teams and individual sportswomen were regularly reported in the press and in the pages of the 'Merchant Maiden'. Off the School site girls enjoyed skiing, both at Hillend and in organised parties in Scotland and abroad, while smaller groups also enjoyed golf and riding. In 1969 the Merchant Company's own Adventure Centre at Ardtrostan House on Loch Earn came into use and gave year groups in both Senior and Junior Schools opportunities to enjoy sailing and canoeing in beauti-

The Swimming Pool

Juniors at Ardtrostan

ful surroundings. The skills learned here were developed with the other Merchant Company Schools on Linlithgow Loch and later at Granton and Queensferry, while hill-walking enjoyed in Perthshire could become a part of Edinburgh life with weekend walking in the Pentlands.

When the School first settled in at Ravelston the secretaries of its various old-established Societies regretfully noted that 'a combination of rain, bus-strikes and the Craigleith drive at 4.30 is enough to discourage the attendance of any Merchant Maiden'. But the girls soon settled into the new pattern of travel by bus and the walk by Blackhall or Craigleith to and from the site and, although on dark winter evenings they walked in groups, some-times accompanied by a Janitor, they soon got used to staying on for Society meetings. The old-established groups, the Literary-Debating, Dramatic and Merchant Maiden Societies, the Missionary Settlement for University Women and Scripture Union groups were supplemented by Edinburgh School Societies such as the Edinburgh Schools' Citizenship Association, the Edinburgh Schools' Scientific Society and the Edinburgh Schools' Classical Society, but facilities at Ravelston, aided by enthusiastic staff support, soon provided a new range of after-school activity. Guides and Brownies continued to be well supported and clubs were formed for enthusiasts in Chess, Photography, Radio, Music, History and Archaeology and Debating with contacts made with other schools for joint lectures and debates. In 1973 the Literary-Debating and Music Societies ran a suc-cessful joint Arts Evening which combined an Art Exhibition with poetry readings and music of the pupils' own composition. Evenings of this kind were often fundraisers and the School's tradition of charitable service continued. Thriving Charities Committees in both Senior and Junior Schools engaged in regular efforts to help a variety of causes from Peter the Polar Bear at Edinburgh Zoo to famine relief and the victims of cancer or spina bifida. These fundraising activities were often on a large scale, raising hundreds of pounds and involving great numbers of enthusiastic girls, happy to follow the School's long tradition of helping those less fortunate than themselves. Practical help was also given at holiday day centres in Edinburgh's deprived areas, in community service and, as a one-off, in delivering mail during a postal strike in 1973.

School trips became an essential part of the year and took girls to places undreamed of in their grandmothers' school days. A visit to Hadrian's Wall and to Rome with the Classics Department became an annual event, as was the long-established exchange with the Victor Duruy Lycée; the Mary Erskine girls continued to enjoy the Paris experience, but returning French pupils often proved un-cooperative in both School and family life and sadly the scheme eventually came to an end. The Modern Languages Department took pupils to France and to Austria while drama was enjoyed at Stratford and at Bradfield. In all this activity there was a great deal of parental support; the School was a lively and exciting place, its reputation was growing and applications for entry always exceeded the places available. The 1970 Centenary was an occasion for real celebration with the Headmistress recalling the events set in motion by the Laurie Report and the appointment of David Pryde.

But away from Ravelston clouds were beginning to gather on the political front. Labour governments were committed to a policy of comprehensive education and to the end of selection in the secondary sector. In 1965 the Scottish Education Department had issued in its Circular 600 a policy statement that all 668 Scottish secondary schools were to become totally comprehensive; the system favoured would be a six-year non-selective system and an end to the paying of fees. 6.5% of Scottish secondary pupils were in fee-paying schools. Some of these were local authority schools which charged minimal fees, but others were completely independent; the largest group, however, was the twenty-nine Grant-Aided Schools which charged fees but were supported by the Scottish Education Department with an annual grant of, at this point, about £114 million. The Edinburgh Grant-Aided Schools included the four Merchant Company foundations, George Heriot's School, Melville College, John Watson's School and St.Mary's Cathedral Choir School, with just over seven thousand pupils. The Merchant Company Schools attracted grant aid of around 40% of their total expenditure which, backed up by their respective investment and endowment incomes, enabled them to keep their fees considerably lower than those in the completely independent sector, making them extremely attractive to parents who sought the best facilities for their children. The Grant-Aided Schools were said to have better classroom facilities, well motivated children, supportive parents and better examination results; at all income levels parents made sacrifices to get their children into such schools, many securing considerable financial support through the endowments and foundations which the Schools offered. Fee-paying Authority Schools and Grant-Aided Schools were not popular with many teachers and administrators in the public sector and were generally accused of creaming off the best of the school population to the disadvantage of both teachers and pupils in the local authority schools. For this reason they were at risk under a Labour administration, and the Education Board in the 1960s was very well aware of the problems ahead. In 1966 the Chairman of the Merchant Company Education Board pointed out that 'education as in 1870 is again in the melting-pot and the Merchant Company should again take the lead', a reference to the policy which had transformed the Merchant Company's Hospitals into Day Schools almost a hundred years earlier.

With this in mind the Board arranged to affiliate itself to the Governing Bodies of the Girls' Schools Association [G.B.G.S.A.] and gave clear information on the various categories of pupils in their Schools who could claim endowment support towards fees. In June, 1967 it issued a statement on the future policy of the Company Schools:

> The Board is reminded of the position in 1870 when their predecessors led educational thought in Scotland. Their first concern now must be the problem of the children in their educational charge and in considering educational changes the Board should lead rather than follow. The Board are very conscious that the Schools cannot live on their past and therefore are ready to consider any reforms which are educationally worthwhile, but are determined to resist any pressure for reform which does not meet the requirements of the children in their charge.[2]

Plans for the future of the Mary Erskine School and Daniel Stewart's College were revealed. There was a firm commitment to single-sex education at the two sites. Extra classrooms were to be provided for each school to house an increased entry at the bottom of the primary departments and a Pavilion and a joint Music Centre would be built at Ravelston to serve them both. These plans anticipated a visit in 1969 by the Public Schools' Commission whose terms of reference in Scotland were to advise on the most effective methods by which Grant-Aided Schools could participate in the movement towards comprehensive reorganisation. The freezing of the grant to Scottish Grant-Aided Schools and to Direct Grant Schools across the border and the abolition of fee-paying in Scottish Authority Schools had already occurred, while a steep teachers' pay rise only added to the Board's problems. A Conservative victory in the election of June, 1970 gave a temporary breathing-space. Hints that the Conservative government was well-disposed towards the Grant-Aided Schools were a relief, but it was necessary for concerted action. A Joint Schools' Working Party [J.S.W.P.] was set up divided into Committees for the North Side (Mary Erskine's and Daniel Stewart's) and the South Side schools (the two George Watson's). In March 1971 representatives of the twenty-nine Scottish Grant-Aided Schools met the Under Secretary for Health and Education over lunch at Merchants' Hall for discussion about their future and set up a central Committee [S.C.O.G.A.S.] of eleven elected delegates whose remit was to negotiate with the Scottish Education Department on all questions connected with the future basis of grant aid. This Committee included the Master and the Secretary and was backed by five regional Committees representing the

Scottish Grant-Aided Schools. The announcement early in 1971 of the restoration of grant aid followed by the news that the grant was to be increased was an immense relief, but the Joint Schools' Working Party in their April Report saw it as no more than temporary:

> It is only now in the light of the welcome statement by the Secretary of State of his intention to increase the amount of grant for the Schools' financial year 1971—2 and subsequent years that it has again become possible to make definite plans for the future development of the Schools. The Conservative administration has made one of its first priorities to restore to education authorities the right to charge fees to a limited number of schools under their management; this should not lead the managers of Grant-Aided Schools to under-estimate the vulnerability of their position. A formula must be found which will enable the Grant-Aided Schools fully to justify their existence as an autonomous assisted group, even to a government opposed in principle to the payment of fees in any school receiving a measure of assistance from public funds. It would be very unwise to acquiesce in a situation which afforded some immediate financial relief to the Grant-Aided Schools if the revised basis of grant aid is one which would be likely to prove unacceptable to an alternative government. There should be no relaxation of the effort to work out a basis for a long-term settlement for the Grant-Aided Schools.[3]

The J.S.W.P. agreed that it would be wise policy to make public the comparative costs of educating a child in an Authority School and one in a Grant-Aided one; the Schools should also plan to introduce a graded fee structure where fees were applied according to the ability to pay them and, most importantly, to initiate discussion with the Local Education Authority 'in accordance with which Grant-Aided Schools would participate in a scheme of coordinated provision of education in the area'. At the same time the North and South Side Committees presented their views on the future of the Schools in their districts. The North Side had five Grant-Aided Schools and just under three thousand pupils concentrated in a small area. In addition to Mary Erskine's and Daniel Stewart's, there were Melville College, John Watson's School and the Cathedral Choir School which were seen as likely to be vulnerable to any future withdrawal of grant support. The specialist school found its own solution, while a 'campus' system to encourage co-operation between the North Side Schools was explored. Discussions on this scheme and on a possible amalgamation of Melville College and John Watson's School with the Company ones brought a definite refusal from the Board of John Watson's School but interest from Melville College, which was eventually to amalgamate with Daniel Stewart's in 1973. The strengthening of the numbers at the new Stewart's Melville made the Board more aware of the weaker position of the Mary Erskine School; with a roll of about five hundred and fifty pupils, an increase of numbers was essential. In his 1972 Report the Master drew attention to this:

> At our oldest educational heritage, the Mary Erskine School, the members of a working party are studying proposals to increase the number of pupils in the Senior School

and to take advantage of the new structure of promoted posts to which the enlarged Schools would become entitled. The Mary Erskine School has prospered under the guidance of Miss Thow. Your Board is presently awaiting the Headmistress' and her colleagues' reports regarding the future. I am confident that whatever advice is offered it will be of high quality, directed towards the best interests of the School.[4]

By the summer of 1973, the roll at the Mary Erskine School was over six hundred and the Principal (the title recently having replaced that of Headmistress) reported that the Promoted Posts system was operating well; she went on to say that:

> Dissatisfaction with the City's policy of non-selection has this year brought many applications which we have been unable to consider. The first year in the Senior School for the autumn of 1973 is already over-subscribed.[5]

However, fee increases were biting and it was reported by the Board that about one-sixth of the parents in their Schools were seeking and receiving assistance towards the payment of fees.

1974 brought problems with two General Elections; the first was inconclusive but the second brought back a stronger Labour administration. At the same time the publication of the Houghton Report on Teachers' Salaries recommended considerable increases at all levels, to be backdated. Anxiously the Scottish Council of Grant-Aided Schools approached the Secretary of the Scottish Education Department, to be informed that no supplementary grant would be available for the 1974—5 session and that the grant would be frozen from 1975. The Education Board's Vice-Chairman and Secretary had talks at Westminster with the Shadow Education Secretary, while non-Labour Scottish M.P.s had sponsored a Commons motion expressing concern at the problems facing the parents of children in Grant-Aided Schools following the grant freeze. For the Board the cost of implementing Houghton's award would mean a serious deficit and a consequent very steep increase in fees, by as much as twenty-five per cent.

In February 1975 about two thousand Merchant Company parents and staff attended a meeting at Stewart's Melville College to hear the Board's future plans for fee rises in the light of the freezing and probable eventual phasing-out of the grant. They were informed that the Board now had only two long-term options: to integrate their Schools into Lothian Region's system or to become fully independent. Six days later a parents' meeting at the Assembly Hall was followed by the formation of a Merchant Company Schools' Parents' Association which joined a consortium representing George Heriot's Trust and John Watson's Trust as pressure groups. The Parents' Association's first Newsletter spelt out the problem:

> Supported by an income derived from investments and from its members, the Merchant Company's total income represents a very small percentage of the size of budget required to finance the running of the three Schools administered by the Merchant Company Education Board. At the present time the Schools' annual expenditure is in

the order of £214 million, of which about 24% is the government grant, now frozen at its 1973 level at which time it represented 40% of the then annual costs.[6]

In June the Education Board, issuing its policy statement for the future of the Schools, said that it had since the second 1974 election held discussions with the Scottish Education Department, with local M.P.s and with representatives of the Region's Education Authority. It had a duty, long-established, to 'hold and administer' the Trusts which had been left by the founders of their three Schools, to allow a degree of parental choice and to offer a flexible system of education. With these points in mind, the Board had decided that three options lay before it: for the Schools to become totally independent of any grant system, to integrate with the Region's education system, or to combine these two options. It had decided

> that integration should be offered at the site of one of the existing Merchant Company Schools and independence at the other two sites. It is proposed that a co-educational school be established on the North side, located either at Ravelston or at Queensferry Road; at the same time it is proposed to negotiate terms on which integration might be offered at one of them.[7]

In June 1975 the parents were informed that the Mary Erskine School would be the 'integrated' one while George Watson's and Stewart's Melville would have 'endowed independence'. The obvious reason for Mary Erskine's selection was that 'from the Region's point of view there was considerable potential for expansion there'. The press announcement about the future of the Mary Erskine School appeared on the day that Jean Thow received a glowing report on the School's performance during an official General Inspection carried out during the summer term.

A questionnaire issued to alarmed parents showed those at Watson's and Stewart's Melville not surprisingly in favour of independence and went on to say, 'there was naturally a strong emotive reaction to the selection of the Mary Erskine School for integration, but this was countered by a measure of relief that the other two Schools had not been selected'. At the Mary Erskine School Jean Thow was besieged by parents anxious to enrol their daughters in a school which would no longer be charging fees. She stated:

> To deny the difficulties outside the School is impossible. The first real blow was the withdrawal at Easter of fifteen VI Formers, theoretically because of an increase of fees. This led after the public examination to withdrawal in Senior V also, something which has never happened before. During the summer term there has been continuous manoeuvring of parents with children in Senior II at Ravelston to transfer their daughters to join brothers at Watson's and of parents at Colinton to allow their daughters to quit the larger school for Ravelston.[8]

Although the Mary Erskine School roll had fallen during the summer term, the numbers were more than made up when places were given to one hundred girls from John Watson's

School which had been forced into closing. About 80% of the Watson's pupils were accommodated in Merchant Company Schools. The Master's comment on these dramatic events and on the rejection of 'the Company's oldest educational heritage' was: 'it is a complex situation and this has been a critical time for many Grant-Aided Schools'.

A shaken Mary Erskine School went home for the summer holidays with many children uncertain of where they would begin the next session. Staff had been assured that after the 1976 takeover there would be no redundancies, that as far as possible primary pupils would be transferred up into the Senior School, that the school uniform would be retained on a voluntary basis under the Region and that the School 'would be allowed to retain its name for six years before being transferred to another Company School'. The School's endowments would be merged with those of the other Company foundations.

In October the Region's Education Councillors met the Under Secretary for Health and Education to ask for borrowing consent and investment allocation to acquire the Mary Erskine School which had been valued at £2.75 million; this was followed by the Region's formal application to central government to borrow the necessary funds. With everything apparently sewn up, a letter on December 10th from the Secretary of State to the Chief Executive of Lothian Region was totally unexpected:

> The Secretary of State has decided that he cannot see his way to meeting at the present time the request of the Regional Council for additional capital investment to enable them to acquire the Mary Erskine School from the Company of Merchants of the City of Edinburgh. The Secretary of State appreciates that the freezing of the grant to the Grant Aided Schools has already caused a sizeable number of pupils to leave these schools and he accepts this process is likely to continue. Places have been found for all the pupils who have so far transferred to the public sector and the Secretary of State is not satisfied that accommodation difficulties are likely to become so acute as to justify at a time of severe financial stringency the very large expenditure of public money that would be required to purchase the Mary Erskine School.[9]

Both the Region and the Merchant Company expressed their reaction in next day's *Scotsman*. The Chairman of Lothian's Education Committee, a prime mover in the battle to integrate the Company's Schools,

> said last night as a furious row started over the government's refusal to provide the cash to carry through their own policies that the position would be so desperate that the Region would have to think about bringing old school buildings in the city into educational use. He could not exclude the old Royal High building. Hundreds of Edinburgh parents would now have to make a difficult choice about their children's future against a background of total confusion. It seemed inevitable that as a result of the government's decision hundreds of parents would be forced to withdraw their children from the Merchant Company Schools.[10]

The Secretary to the Merchant Company was equally outspoken:

One is left in serious doubt about the validity of the government's policy. The Region has already absorbed five hundred pupils from Grant Aided Schools. The Mary Erskine School would have provided roughly one thousand desperately needed secondary places. I (*sic*) had hoped to get two hundred and fifty each from Craigmount and the Royal High into the Mary Erskine School. I despair of the government's logic.[11]

More reasoned comment was provided in the *Scotsman's* editorial comment:

The fiasco is of more than local significance. As part of their imaginary 'mandate' from a handful of voters in last year's general election the government commenced the phasing-out of grants. Lothian Region and the Merchant Company duly made their plans to cope with the government's policy, the Region with some relish, the Merchant

---

NOSTALGIA

Clusters of pink and green and blue,
Clusters of tables, clusters of people,
Plastic and new.

Standing, sitting, kneeling, talking,
They're Making Things—it's Self Expression.
Some get up to go and have a look at someone else's,
And no one stops them.
Or they're doing equations with rainbow rods,
Or watching the birds from the classroom window,
And the atmosphere's alive
With industry,
And interest,
And freedom.

But we sat in straight brown rows of wooden desks.
And we sat still and quiet,
And counted with red counters,
And had to put our hands up,
And expressed what others wanted.
We were pink and breen and blue;
Just the same,
Only different.

SUSAN MYERSCOUGH, VS.

Nostalgia

Company reluctantly. There has been no shortage among Labour's ruling class of missionary zeal to impose their dogma on an unwilling nation. We are probably to have three independent schools all catering for parents who are rich enough to meet the fees while an unexpectedly large number of children whose parents cannot meet these fees are thrown into an overcrowded state system.[12]

The ball was back in the Merchant Company's court.

REFERENCES

1   JEAN THOW, 10.1.1967.
2   EDUCATION BOARD LEAFLET, 8.6.1967.
3   J.S.W.P. REPORT, 29.4.1971.
4   MASTER'S REPORT, 1972.
5   JEAN THOW, REPORT, 1973.
6   M.C.S.P.A. NEWSLETTER, FEBRUARY, 1975.
7   E.B.M., JUNE, 1975.
8   JEAN THOW, REPORT, 1975.
9   W. HUTCHISON TO THE CHIEF EXECUTIVE, LOTHIAN REGION, 10.12.1975.
10–12   *SCOTSMAN*, 11.12.1975.

Robin Morgan

'New Days, New Ways'

In January 1976 Lothian Region, in a last attempt to secure the Mary Erskine School, petitioned the Secretary of State for Scotland for permission to enter into an annuity arrangement over a twenty-five-year period; when this was refused the Secretary to the Education Board announced to the parents that the School, like George Watson's and Stewart's Melville, would be maintained on an 'endowed independence' basis. In order to ensure the survival of the three schools without staggering fee rises an Appeal would be launched in the autumn to raise an Endowment Fund of one million pounds for them all.

In her Annual Report for the session 1975—1976 Jean Thow spoke with feeling of the session just over:

> The academic year has consisted of two rather than three terms, the great divide occur-
> ring somewhere in the no-man's-time between December 12th, 1975 and January 15th,
> 1976. The first half of the year was rough; the second has not been smooth [but] the
> year will be a vintage year in achievements.[1]

The events of the previous year had taught the Education Board some valuable lessons. The strength and bargaining power of the Parents' Association and expectations of regular discussion from the Merchant Company Teachers' Association meant that it must emerge from Olympian seclusion and begin to talk to those who paid the fees and those in their employ. Parents in Grant-Aided Schools were beginning to question the composition of School Boards with no parental representation on them. The days when parents were grateful to have their children admitted to such schools were over. The Boards were now going to have to fight in an increasingly competitive market to attract and to keep customers, not only by providing the traditional high academic standards in a disciplined milieu but also by offering amenities of a standard undreamed of in the days of assured grant aid and low fees. Boards and Principals would in future have to become adept in the public relations field, selling their Schools in a value-conscious market with the same skills that were already traditional in the world of business which was the backbone of the

Merchant Company.

With all this in mind the Education Board moved fast to co-opt a member of the Merchant Company Parents' Association. In May, 1976 they went on to appoint as the new Principal of Stewart's Melville a candidate who fulfilled their need for a good public relations man. Robin Morgan was already known to them, having taught in George Watson's before becoming Principal of Campbell College, Belfast. Scots by birth, a graduate of Aberdeen University, his National Service years had stamped him with a love of things military which was shown in his strong belief in a Combined Cadet Force as an essential adjunct to school life and character training. Accustomed to command, he was a strong disciplinarian with a dislike of sloppiness in appearance or behaviour, while his obvious skills in committee and ability to communicate with business and professional interests would make him an essential agent in the drive to promote the public image of the School. He took up office in January, 1977, closing an eighteen months' interregnum at Stewart's Melville.

The Parents' Association was now giving very real background support in the School, proposing an Open Evening and an Open Day to attract a wider public and planning a Thrift Shop for the sale of outgrown uniforms and equipment. In May 1977 Parents' Meetings at the three Schools attracted large numbers, but behind the scenes the Joint Schools' Working Party was looking nervously at admission applications for the next session. The North Side group reported that applications were down for P7 admission at both Mary Erskine's and Stewart's Melville; numbers at Mary Erskine's had fallen by about one hundred, resulting in a considerable deficit for the session. A generous bequest of £25,000 from a former pupil would not help the situation, as it was specifically earmarked for scholarship endowment. The Joint Schools' Working Party in meetings during the course of the summer term discussed several plans. Although the members correctly identified the problems of loss of grant and of falling numbers, they failed to agree on a solution and their findings were presented to the Education Board in September. They did not support the proposal put forward by Jean Thow and her Vice-Convener that the Mary Erskine School should operate in future as an independent unit of about eight hundred and fifty pupils with its own Management Committee, Bursar and fee structure and with the ability to offer foundations and fee remissions from its endowment income. The proponents of this plan believed that, although an initial loss would certainly be sustained, there was no reason why it could not eventually be made good and that the School would be a viable unit. Also presented was a plan to merge Mary Erskine's and Daniel Stewart's by degrees into a combined unit of around thirteen hundred pupils, beginning with a Junior School merger in September 1978 and the gradual extension of a 'twinning' system to the Senior departments. For three years the Schools were to operate on both sites; then it might be possible to house the complete School at Stewart's Melville, again offering the Ravelston site to Lothian Region. Girls whose parents wished them to remain in a Merchant Company School would be offered places either at Stewart's Melville or at George Watson's. The 'twinning' process on which the two Senior Schools would embark would involve a common curriculum, shared facilities and a joint Principal. Fees for the first year of Primary entry should be kept as low as possible to attract admissions, but Senior School fees must inevitably rise. At this juncture the Education Board took no decision and the Joint Schools' Working Party was never re-convened. It was not until January 1978 that something of a revision of this proposal re-emerged.

The Board accepted this proposal in principle as far as the immediate merging of the two Junior Schools was concerned. It was estimated that considerable savings could be made by accommodating the Primary Grades on one chosen site. Although accommodation was already available at Mary Erskine's, temporary classrooms were hastily erected at Stewart's Melville for the establishment of the Combined Junior School for the new 1978 session. A staffing committee for the new unit was set up. The Principals of both Schools pleaded on educational grounds for a merger of Primary 1—5 only, while parents of girls in Primary 4 refused to allow their daughters to transfer for only a year to the other site. At Ravelston a feeder Nursery was opened in the now empty Primary classrooms.

Many parents and staff were unhappy about these proposals, feeling that there had been a lack of consultation with them and also with the Schools' Principals. The Merchant Company Parents' Association pointed out that there was a real demand in Edinburgh for single-sex education and felt that the Board was being unduly pessimistic about the ability of parents to find the fees for the type of schooling they wanted for their children. Publicity for the Schools was essential.

The virtues of close co-operation within a complementary group of schools, the maintenance of academic standards rooted in the Scottish system, the development of a sense of community between the Schools and the family and shared outdoor activities were all selling points. It was felt also that there should be much closer contact between the Board and the parents:

> In the past in general parents have been tolerated but not encouraged. There is every incentive in the schools, indeed it is essential for their survival, positively to welcome and encourage potential and existing parents to see the schools at work and play. Very much more could be done to involve parents in school activities, including the use of sports facilities. Parents will come to realise that they are not just providers of cash to finance their children's school education; when they start their children in a Merchant Company school they will be joining a community.[2]

The Merchant Company Teachers' Association, the Former Pupils' Guild and countless individual parents also expressed concern to the Board that neither they nor the Principals had been involved or consulted enough in recent important decisions which would profoundly affect them all. The three Principals had been members of the Joint Schools' Working Party until September, 1977. After that date, whatever discussions might have been held privately, one Principal at least felt that she had been kept in the dark. When, in March 1978, the Principals of George Watson's and of Stewart's Melville both refuted the charge of lack of consultation in a letter of support to the Education Board's policy, Jean Thow refused to add her signature to their letter, giving her reasons for this in a separate letter to the Education Board:

> Since September, 1977, there was no working party or forum of any kind for joint discussion of the [merger] plan. In my view, on the information that I have to date been given on the P1—P5 merger of the North Side schools on the Stewart's Melville site, it is against the best interests of the Mary Erskine School and also, in so far that the Principal of one school can make judgements about another school, of Stewart's Melville and therefore of the three schools as a group. Nevertheless, as Principal of the Mary Erskine school at the pleasure of the Education Board, I am entrusted to the implementing of the Board's decisions and will continue as I have in the past to carry out the instructions in both the spirit and the letter of their intention.[3]

In May a statement from the Chairman of the Parents' Association addressed the whole question of liaison between the Board and the parents, Principals and staff and suggested that it should be the policy of the Board to admit the Principals to its meetings. With the Combined Junior School's arrival due in the autumn, Robin Morgan issued a Parents' Newsletter on the benefits of twinning and reported on his school's summer Open Day which had been attended by many prospective entrants:

> Male phlegmatism collapsed under the assault of so much cheerful charm and skilfully deployed femininity. The effect of a gap-toothed smile in the midst of an aureole of blonde or brunette curls is devastating. Those who attended our Open Day and witnessed the little girls hunting our little boys in packs know who has taken over whom.[4]

At Mary Erskine's Jean Thow in her Annual Report to the Merchant Company Education Board complimented her staff and her school:

> It is a tribute to the Staff that they have maintained their interest in students and in research projects and that high standards in school work, the arts and sport have again been achieved in a year when the morale of the school, not yet recovered from the 1975 upheaval, has been constantly undermined by rumour, uncertainty and lack of external confidence. This could have broken a staff which was not secure in its own competence and one which is fully capable of making its own judgements. One said, 'We trained hard but it seemed that every time we were beginning to form up into teams we would be reorganised.' Reorganising is a wonderful method for creating the illusion of progress while producing confusion, inefficiency and demoralisation. There is a widespread feeling that the humanity and simple courtesy, formerly so characteristic of all activities in Merchant Company Schools, have been lost. Mary Erskine's School is at present like a vine which has been severed from its root. We remain to see whether the delicate process of grafting onto a new base will take, as we hope it will.[5]

At the end of the summer term parents at both Schools received a letter from the Merchant Company Board, outlining its proposals for the coming session:

Combined Junior School Pupils

It has been decided to appoint one Principal in overall charge of both schools with the intention of retaining the services of both Miss Jean Thow and Mr.Robin M. Morgan. Both Principals have been invited to express an interest in the new post of Principal on the understanding that the alternative post will be that of an Associate Principal or Headmistress/master. The Education Board feels that this will be in the best interest of both schools and reaffirms its intention to retain the Mary Erskine School and Daniel Stewart's and Melville College as two separate single-sex schools from Primary 6 upwards.[6]

In September letters to both parents and staff announced that from the beginning of October Robin Morgan was to be in overall charge of the two North Side Schools and that Jean Thow would be the Headmistress of the Mary Erskine School. From the middle of the autumn term of 1978 the girls' School found itself in the confusing position of apparently having two Principals. On two days a week Robin Morgan was on the site, establishing his study in the big former Library of Ravelston House, taking Morning Assembly, interviewing individual staff and groups of Prefects and inviting parents to come to him for discussion on any problems affecting their daughters. On the other three days Jean Thow appeared to be in control, operating from her usual office in the new block and carrying out her normal duties.

An introductory Staff Meeting had been held and the Headmistress had introduced the new Principal who had outlined to them his plans for the future re-organisation of the school. Much consideration was being given to join activities with Stewart's Melville and he had identified areas in Mary Erskine's which must be reviewed at an early date. These included the structure of the promoted posts scheme, the guidance system and discipline within the school. A new timetable would be drawn up to parallel that in use at Stewart's Melville, discussions would be held about the possibility of replacing the Mary Erskine system of streaming classes with the setting system in use at the other school, plans were being made for joint classes to be established in some subjects and girls would be given the opportunity to participate with the boys, not only as at present in Music and Drama, but also in outdoor activities such as the Carbisdale Project and in joining the Combined Cadet Force. Parents would be issued with frequent Newsletters to keep them in touch with what was going on in the two schools and a new Prospectus would be issued. He reported to the Board that 'The staff had given him positive support and encouragement'.

The Staff were genuinely ready to be supportive and encouraging but they were at this stage as confused as the girls. Things had moved too fast; there had been no preparation for the sweeping changes that were being outlined to them with so much enthusiasm and they were finding themselves torn between conflicting loyalties. They had worked for eleven years with Jean Thow and respected her as an able administrator and a caring colleague; now they saw her relegated to a position without apparent responsibility, subject like them to orders from a higher authority which seemed determined to stamp the Mary Erskine School with a Stewart's Melville identity. Things were not made easy by the apparent insensitivity with which they and the Headmistress were treated. Confident in a man's world, the new Principal did not find it easy to communicate with professional women; faced with a situation which would have daunted anyone and which must have seemed to him like walking into the lionesses' den, he reacted by being brusquely directive or by making complimentary remarks which often raised feminist hackles. He found it easier to avoid group confrontation and preferred individual interviews. The Staff became accustomed to the arrival of written comunications from the Principal's bunker, outlining areas in which they were seen as failing to come up to scratch; tersely worded, these were often wounding and did not help a situation which was difficult on both sides. In time it became apparent that the Principal had a short fuse but that at heart he was, as he would say himself, 'an old softie'. On bad days lesser heads were kept well below the parapet and those who worked closest with him learned to proffer coffee and sympathy.

The two-headed administration of the school was obviously doomed to failure from the start. A pair of saints would have found it impossible to operate the system, and temperamentally the two who had been forced into this impossible situation could never make it work. Robin Morgan had his orders from the Board and had as soon as possible to show that the new system was workable; with the help of his own Stewart's Melville staff rapid changes were carried out. Jean Thow, relegated to a position without real authority, was expected to accept these changes and to encourage her staff to implement them. She had informed the Board on Robin Morgan's appointment that she would 'continue as Headmistress to carry out her duties and obligations'; but she found the process of rapid change distasteful and unacceptable and fought hard to ease the process for her girls and for her staff. Inevitably this brought her into conflict with the new Principal who saw her as uncooperative and reported the situation regularly to the Board where he and the Principal of George Watson's now attended certain meetings. The Education Board could not do other than support the Principal whom they had appointed, and Jean Thow came under increasing pressure from the Master to resign. Having attended her last Prize-Giving, seated on the stage while her successor outlined the School's progress during the session just ended, she agreed to demit office after a year's leave of absence. This she used to wind up the Headship of the Mary Erskine School and all the professional and educational associations which accrued from it. Her concern was that the good name of the School should not be tarnished in any significant areas.

In his report for 1978—1979 Robin Morgan spoke of the changes envisaged for the Mary Erskine School:

> To meet the needs and perplexities of a changing, more complex and often very confusing society, a new system of pastoral, curricular and careers guidance has been grafted onto the corporate body of the school. Great attention is being paid to the girls' recreational needs and the school day has been reorganised to enable them to engage more widely in cultural and sporting activities. Twinning policy has been seen at Carbisdale, in the Combined Cadet Force and at joint concerts. The first Corps camp is to be held on my mother-in-law's estate in Wester Ross and two of the girls will be with me at Bisley, disarming the opposition with their charm and putting them off their aim. The uncertainties, the misgivings of the past are of the past, finished, over and done with.[7]

On the first day of the new session the Staff and parents heard for the first time of Jean Thow's departure from the School.

With Jean Thow's retirement the position of Headmistress of the Mary Erskine School lapsed; instead the Education Board appointed a Deputy-Principal from the Staff who would do much to ease tension during the early months of 1980 and who would prove invaluable to Robin Morgan during his years at Ravelston. The coming decade was a time of rapid growth and change which the girls accepted as natural but which found Staff and parents sometimes almost breathless as they watched the School's response to the fast-moving world of the '80s. Robin Morgan made no secret of his happiness in his role as Head of a girls' school; the girls in turn responded to the continual challenges and to his pride in their achievements. He was never happier than in presenting his annual Prize-Giving Report on the girls' achievements with a panache which sometimes raised eyebrows but which was part of his persona:

> We stand at the end of a session of prodigious activity. It must be a very long time since so many girls were involved in music, drama, dance, games and athletics, hill-walking, adventure training, canoeing, sailing, flying, sewing and stitching. It's such a long list that reciting it leaves one as breathless and enfeebled as any of the young ladies who, in the merry month of May, staggered to the top of Ben More Assynt as part of the programme of outdoor education we arranged for them at Carbisdale. It was for me a

fascinating experience to see some of those dishevelled and pitiable urchins who had crawled into Croick or tottered down to Inchnadamph transformed at our Dancing Display into dazzling disco queens, mob-capped country lasses and dancers of something called the Blackbottom. Was that young courtier who danced the Galliard with such exquisite grace the same girl who last year stood, her hair streaming in the wind, on the crest of the ridge above Strathcarron? And surely the enchanting bride of the 'Wedding Ring' couldn't be the same girl as the one who parades in naval uniform down at Stewart's Melville on Monday afternoons? Some would argue that the Principal of the Mary Erskine School should by this time be impervious to surprise, that the news that a Mary Erskine girl has discovered the elixir of youth or the Philosopher's Stone should produce not so much as a flicker of his well-groomed eyebrows. Give me time and no doubt I'll cultivate a positively Wellingtonian sang-froid [but] versatility, the capacity to turn one's hand to the most diverse pursuits, coupled with a striving after perfection, would seem to be the twin key-notes of the School.[8]

The Principal loved to stress the duality of his girls, their combination of feminine graces and skills and a toughness, both physical and intellectual, which could rival that of the boys at Stewart's Melville. He was determined that the two Schools should remain separate entities each with its own unique character, but many of the pupils had come up together through the Combined Junior School and twinning was to be encouraged in as many joint activities as possible. Music and drama had been shared for some years; now there was to be inter-school cooperation both in and out of the classroom. To a Principal devoted to things military and to the outdoor life there were obvious areas where the girls' extra-curricular horizons could be expanded, notably in Adventure Training and in the Combined Cadet Force. From 1980 each May saw the departure of the Third Years of the two schools to Carbisdale Castle Youth Hostel for nine days of joint hill-walking, orienteering, canoeing and environmental studies. In an exercise run with military efficiency, over two hundred children and a large accompanying staff were bussed north to embark on a unique experience. Some might have expected it to be a holiday but soon they would all discover the demands which these days and nights of community life and physical effort would make:

> I really enjoyed canoeing in the dark and sleeping under the stars. I would do it again any time.
> I had imagined Carbisdale to be a kind of holiday, but my views were soon shattered when we began the 'Duke of Edinburgh' walk. The weather was unpredictable, one minute sun and the next snow! Despite the weather we bravely battled our way through streams, bogs and forests. We collapsed often, but our first stop was caused by a fit of hysterics. One of the boys, while plodding through the heather, had not noticed the bog and slowly began to sink. From then on the atmosphere was superb. We laughed and moaned but even when we complained we enjoyed it. Walking the nine kilometers to Croick was not exactly enjoyable but it did give me some feeling of independence, though it is hard to be independent when you're up to your knees in a peat bog with a two-ton rucksack on your back.

Carbisdale

I was delighted that I had reached the top of Ben More Assynt because it had been a very strenuous climb. It was worth it, however, because we had a fantastic view over the surrounding countryside and right out to sea. Further down the slopes we saw some deer running. After miles and miles of breathtaking walks up and down steep rocky mountains my throat got really dried out and water had never tasted so fantastic in my life before. I had never had the chance to climb a mountain before and I was very proud of my achievement.[9]

Carbisdale Castle, a vast nineteenth-century pile with unheated panelled rooms, plate glass windows, minimal washing facilities and an improbable collection of nude marble statuary, was totally unsuited for Youth Hostel use, but this was all part of the experience:

The castle was a magic place. There were paintings hanging perilously from the walls and life-like statues parading daringly down the hall. The uncarpeted floors, cold rooms and cold showers all added to the splendour of the Castle. Although being awakened by bagpipes at seven in the morning was not very good fun, it did clear my brain ready for another day's adventures. From the day we left to the day we came back it was like a dream because it passed so quickly and yet we did so much. I made lots of new friends and everybody learned to pull together as a team in all the triumphs and troubles we had.[10]

Friendships forged at Carbisdale, and later also at its Strathpeffer annexe, could be strengthened back in Edinburgh. The girls in Third Year were encouraged to become members of the Combined Cadet Force at Stewart's Melville in Army, Navy or Air Force sections. Within two years Robin Morgan could boast that his was the only girls' school in the country with C.C.F. members who were not only parading weekly with the boys but, as highland dancers, were joining the Pipe Band for demonstrations. In time this would lead to goodwill foreign tours to France and Sardinia, while the Principal's happiest moments came when he accompanied his girls' shooting teams to Bisley and triumphantly escorted them home again with their trophies. Younger pupils were broken in gently for Carbisdale with summer-term Projects, again shared with their peers at Stewart's Melville; canoeing, orienteering, art, history and environmental studies gave a week of shared companionship and of new experiences:

R.A.F. section, Combined Cadet Force

For those with strong stomachs there was a merry seven hour coach trip to Hadrian's Wall and back again; if you felt like being cultured at the Burrell Collection or seeing Billy Connolly's banana boots at the People's Palace there was an even merrier excursion to Glasgow; for perfect blisters, fallen arches or corns a hearty walk in the Pentlands was included; there was a swim in the Forth at Port Edgar for those who thought they were going canoeing or sailing; and finally at Beecraigs you could abseil, mountain-bike, pioneer, orienteer, arch[ery], rock climb and at the end expire! So much for a week off! Actually these projects were really good.[11]

Reading the 'Merchant Maiden' for the '80s often gives the impression that the girls were rarely in School, such was their range of expeditions and trips to Rome for classical study, to London and Paris with the Art Department, to London again for Politics and to Paris again for History, to Holland with the hockey team or the C.C.F., to Stratford and Bradfield and Pitlochry for Drama, to Italy and Switzerland for skiing, Brittany for French, to the Mediterranean on school cruises and to the United States with Operation Friendship. Individual girls went further afield for even more adventurous expeditions: to Papua New Guinea and the Antarctic with the British Schools' Exploring Society, using a Kenneth Ryden Travel Scholarship as a means to work in a Salvation Army Hospital in Zambia, participating in the Tall Ships sailing race, or playing chess for Scotland in Romania. Such trips cost money, often more than parents could afford, and a great deal

Music making

of busy fundraising went on throughout the year. This did not put a stop to the charity fundraising which had been part of the School since its early days. An active Charities' Committee encouraged such activities on a scale far removed from the old 'penny a week' class contributions; in 1983 girls in the History Department raised £100 to endow a prize, in 1984 £700 was raised for a kidney dialysis machine, and by 1989 a joint Schools' Technology Appeal by pupils, staff and parents could raise £24,000 in a day. The skills of all those participating had been honed by years of smaller-scale charity work.

In the background finance was much in the minds of the Board, the parents and the Principal. The lessons of 1975 had been learned: any change of government could mean

Early days in Computer Studies

the end of grant aid. In December, 1979, George Younger spoke at Merchants' Hall to the representatives of the Scottish Grant-Aided Schools, outlining his government's future plans for the 1981 Education (Scotland) Bill. By this grant aid would be phased out and would be replaced by the Assisted Places Scheme. By 1981, nineteen Scottish Grant-Aided Schools were ready to participate in a scheme whereby children over the age of eleven could be eligible for fee assistance for five years if their parents' annual income was less than nine thousand pounds. The Bill would, when ratified, require all former Grant-Aided Schools to register as independent and, unlike the Authority Schools, to pay their own examination fees. Cushioned by these financial reassurances, supplemented by endowment income and by funds raised through land sales, the Board felt that the Schools' future was for the time being secure. Senior School fees were by now well over one thousand pounds a year in the Senior Schools, but parents still managed somehow to raise the necessary money. Income in commercial and professional circles was rising, grandparents' covenant schemes were becoming common, and highly skilled working wives provided additional funding for their children's education. Fee administration had become more complicated with the reckoning needed for the Assisted Places Scheme. The Board moved into the technological age and bought its first fee-processing computer.

It was important to publicise the Schools' Assisted Places Scheme and their other amenities. New prospectuses drew attention to Scholarship, Foundation and Bursary provision, to the recent opening by Lady Mar and Kellie of a Mary Erskine boarding house at 7/9 Queensferry Terrace and to the development of Computer Studies in the School. The Home Economics Department in Ravelton House had been completely upgraded at a cost of £56,000, a changing pavilion built for the boys who used the Ravelston site for sports and swimming and a new all-weather games pitch laid out. All this activity coincided with 1981's most important activity, the celebration of the Merchant Company's Tercentenary.

Plans for marking this important date had been long in the making. The Company would hold a combined Tercentenary and Kirking service at St.Giles' followed by a civic reception from the City of Edinburgh. In July there would be a royal visit to Merchants' Hall. A film about the Company's history and activities would be made, a special exhibition held at Peterhead and a dance given to all the Staff. A Schools' Committee drew up plans for a programme of celebration. At Mary Erskine's this included a Dance Display, a Chamber Concert in an intimate setting, a Claret by Candlelight evening with music and food of the period served by costumed waitresses and an exhibition of life at Ravelston in the 1680s. The celebrations ended with a grand fireworks display.

The most lasting memorials of the Tercentenary are two pieces of work still displayed in the School beside its greatest treasure, the Mary Erskine table carpet. It was the suggestion of the History Department that the School might produce, as a gift to the Merchant Company, a pendant to the earlier piece to demonstrate contemporary skills in

The Boarding House

needlework. Designed by the Home Economics Department, eventually two pieces of work were donated to the Company with one proviso: that they were to hang not at the Merchants' Hall but in the School as a reminder to future generations of their 'Founders and Benefactors'. The larger piece, symbolic of the Merchant Company's role in Edinburgh history, shows the Company galleon afloat on a broad river, backed by the hills of Fife; the smaller panel in a more naive style depicts the Master, Secretary and Treasurer of 1981, modern school pupils and Merchants of past years posed against a background of the four Halls used by the Company in its three-hundred-year history. To show that it was a gift from the School as a whole, every person in the building, Principal, Staff, girls of all ages, secretaries, janitors and domestic staff, right down to the youngest pupil, was asked to put at least one stitch into the pieces; many girls and staff did much more than this and took great pleasure in watching the pieces grow. They were brought to Merchants' Hall to be shown to the Queen and the Duke of Edinburgh during the royal visit when two of the 'sewing girls' were invited to explain the work.

Academically the school was in good heart. The new Standard Grade syllabus was gradually introduced from 1987, but S.C.E. Higher and Sixth Year Studies courses were still the goal of fifth- and sixth-year girls and became increasingly popular. The Sixth Form remained a large one, usually well over sixty girls, sharing some of their courses with boys from Stewart's Melville. Around seventy per cent of the Sixth would go on to further education at University or College in Scotland and England. A growing number chose Oxbridge entry, encouraged by the Principal who arranged exploratory group visits to Colleges and discussions with Admissions Tutors. The careers chosen by leavers became more varied, helped by the development of careers advice at various stages in school life and by the introduction of a computerised careers advice scheme. Consumer studies, civil engineering, recreational management, land economy and biochemistry joined the more conventional career options, helped by work experience schemes for fifth-year girls and by Young Enterprise schemes to give production and marketing training. Careers advice and general school support were also given at all levels by the School's Guidance staff, reorganised by the Principal on a Clan rather than Year basis. The four original clan names of Erskine, Hopetoun, Marischal and Mar still survived. The School Guidance structure was also re-arranged with the appointment of new posts of Heads of Upper and Middle Schools.

The 1980s saw other anniversaries; the 350th anniversary of the birth of Mary Erskine was marked by the Former Pupils' Guild with the presentation to the School of an Alison Geissler engraved goblet. In 1984 the Guild celebrated its own Centenary with a year of celebration and reminiscence. A pair of decanters, again engraved by Mrs.Geissler, was the School's gift, coupled with a commemorative sampler from the Staff to its former pupils; the Merchant Company at the Guild's Centenary dinner made a presentation of an engraved silver lectern. In return the Former Pupils laid out a Heather Garden in the grounds at Ravelston during the winter of 1983, formally presenting it to the School on Founders' Day, 1984; a week later a special Reunion in the School was marked by exhibitions of Art and of the School's history. A special Centenary Service of Thanksgiving at

Greyfriars' was followed by a visit to the plaque commemorating Mary Erskine's burial in the graveyard. Since the 1960s a plot in the Covenanters' Prison had been marked with the Founder's name, a white rose tree and a bush of broom, and the tradition had grown up that representatives of the School and the Guild should visit the site in June each year; in 1984 this ceremony was marked by a special service.

During the 1980s the Schools consolidated their reputation for joint productions in music and drama. The Juniors were included in Edinburgh Festival performances of *Noye's Fludde* and *The Tower of Babel* and a series of musical and dramatic events in the Schools developed their reputation as young singers, players and actors. The Seniors' productions drew on the skills of the Art, Music and Home Economics Departments in increasingly lavish and professional productions, whether in drama with *Le Bourgeois Gentilhomme* and *The Business of Good Government* or in musicals such as *The Boy Friend* and *Guys and Dolls*. Music, orchestral and vocal, punctuated the school year; choirs, madrigal groups, orchestras and wind bands celebrated special occasions like Founders' Day, gave concerts and recitals to parents and guests and came together in St.Mary's Cathedral for a joyful Christmas Carol Service. The School continued to enjoy a variety of options in Sport far beyond the traditional Hockey, Netball and Tennis. These included skiing, curling, athletics and weight-training, while gymnastics and dance reached high performance standards.

In 1988 plans began to be made to bring Mary Erskine's and Stewart's Melville up to date with the introduction of Technology courses for both girls and boys. A million-pound appeal was launched, set off to a good start with the Education Board's initial donation of

Brecht on Stage

£75,000. Enthusiastic support from the parents supplemented generous gifts from corporate donors. An imaginative range of fundraising efforts included sponsored mountaineering, an Antiques Roadshow and a performance of the *Snowman*, culminating in an all-day Carnival at Ravelston involving hundreds of parents, pupils and staff which raised thousands of pounds. With three quarters of a million promised, building could begin on both sites by 1989. The same year saw change in the Schools' management with the proposal to establish new Governing Boards under whose able and concerned administration the future now looked secure. It was also marked by Robin Morgan's retiral as Principal of the North Side Schools.

In his last report he looked back over his eleven years as Principal of Mary Erskine's:

> When I took over the Mary Erskine School I had my fair share of misconception about girls and girls' schools. I have jettisoned them all. I am a complete convert to the Mary Erskine brand of feminism, that is a blend of quite militant sex egalitarianism with a gracious femininity. My girls are all perfect ladies until you suggest that they are in any way at all inferior to the boys. I am so proud of my girls. They have never fallen short of my increasing expectations of them. They have never let me down.[12]

Eileen McCamley, the Deputy-Principal who had worked so closely with him over the years, summed up his achievements:

Bisley

The task which the Education Board gave him in 1978 was to implement its policy of 'twinning' its two North Side schools. While preserving the separate identities and the long traditions of both schools, he was to forge links which would be to their mutual advantage and explore and exploit possibilities for widening the educational, social and cultural experience of their pupils.

Such a task demanded energy, enthusiasm, imagination, entrepreneurial gifts and a distinct flair for public relations. Add to these qualities a sense of humour, spontaneity and a swashbuckling style, offset by approachability and a paternalistic warmth and you have the man the Education Board found for the job to be done.

When asked how he saw his role as Principal, he unhesitatingly replied that it was first and foremost a pastoral one and it was this pastoral emphasis which led him to make himself accessible and to take a personal interest in so many individuals. He enjoyed the company of his Merchant Maidens and was receptive to their ideas and sympathetic to their problems. Should all else be forgotten the memory of a bon viveur, a witty raconteur and Highland laird manqué, striding off — faithful dogs at heel — into the woods at Ravelston will remain.[13]

REFERENCES

1   JEAN THOW, PRINCIPAL'S REPORT, 1976.
2   E.B.M., 1978, APPENDIX 78/17.
3   JEAN THOW TO EDUCATION BOARD, MARCH 27TH, 1978.
4   ROBIN MORGAN, PRINCIPAL'S REPORT (D.S.M.C.),1978.
5   JEAN THOW, PRINCIPAL'S REPORT, 1978.
6   E.B.M., JUNE, 1978.
7   ROBIN MORGAN, PRINCIPAL'S REPORT (M.E.S.G.), 1979.
8   ROBIN MORGAN, PRINCIPAL'S REPORT, 1981.
9   M.M., 1981.
10   M.M., 1989.
11   M.M., 1989.
12   ROBIN MORGAN, PRINCIPAL'S REPORT, 1989
13   N.M., 1989.

Patrick Tobin

R obin Morgan's successor was the first Englishman to be entrusted with the leadership of the School. A schoolmaster for twenty-six years, Patrick Tobin had been since 1981 the first lay headmaster of Prior Park College in Bath. In that capacity he had introduced girls to a previously single-sex boys' school. He had also been active in the transfer of the management of a school from central control by a religious order to a new Governing Council. That process was to be repeated in the Edinburgh Merchant Company schools shortly after his arrival.

This revolution in the Merchant Company's management of its schools was the achievement of the outgoing Master, Michael Walker. He perceived that the logic of Independent education was that schools should be empowered to take genuine responsibility for the conduct and planning of their own affairs. The events of the 1970s had demonstrated the shortcomings of the 'ancien régime' at Hanover Street; since then, Principal and teaching staff alike had chafed against the restrictions on initiative and communication which this system engendered. Not the least of Patrick Tobin's responsibilities was the transfer of administrative and strategic accountability from Hanover Street to the schools.

On the eve of his first session he spoke to the teaching staff:

> I am acutely aware that this is not *any* Head's job! Indeed, I am not aware of any counterpart in the British Independent sector. I am already conscious of a strong vein of sympathetic tolerance among my senior colleagues and I trust that this admirable sentiment will endure, for a while at least.

> What is very clear to me is that it is incumbent on me to conduct the orchestra, and also to ensure that the three orchestras can come together to play as one. In the past this role was, in a sense, shared between the Principal and the Education Board, Secretary and Deputy Secretary of the Merchant Company. Now the umbilical link with Merchants' Hall will, if you like, be cut. Our Siamese twinship with George

Watson's College is, to a degree at least, at an end. The Bursarial, Maintenance and Catering functions are firmly within the Principal's purview, not outside it.

While the new arrangements conferred freedom on the school and on its leaders, they inevitably imposed human limitations on the Principal. None of his predecessors had had to take over two schools at once and none had been expected to play the role of 'chief executive'. He would gain in accountability, but there would be a cost in terms of personal contact, especially with the pupils. His reference to 'three' schools indicated a conscious decision to delegate greater autonomy to the able new Headmaster of the Junior School, Bryan Lewis.

On November 16th, 1989 the Erskine Stewart's Melville Governing Council came formally into being. It had already reached important decisions with regard to the future structure of the three schools. The trigger for this rapid decision was the success of the 1988 Technology Appeal, which Bryan Lewis had personally directed. This appeal had begged all sorts of questions. What exactly was Technology? Should it 'happen' at both ends of Ravelston Dykes, or should it be centred on one site? If a major new dimension was to be introduced into the school curriculum, would it be necessary to eliminate or reduce other elements? Underlying all these questions was a more fundamental one. Was the current structure of the schools to endure for the foreseeable future?

With impressive speed and decisiveness the new Governing Council approved the proposal that the girls and boys of the Junior School should remain together at Queensferry Road until the end of Primary 7. This would be achieved by the building of a new classroom block for the Nursery and Preparatory Department at Ravelston, so that all girls and boys would be taught on the Mary Erskine site up to the end of Primary 3. Nor was this all. The Bursar's offices, originally intended for Queensferry Terrace, would also be established at Ravelston.

The effect of these changes on the Mary Erskine School was to be significant. Robin Morgan had trumpeted the virtues of the school from the rooftops, but the staff who had worked under Jean Thow would not have been human had they not seen 'twinning' as a form of Queensferry Road imperialism. The more apprehensive, indeed, might well have wondered what changes the new Principal would introduce, when the previous twenty-five years had witnessed such bewildering and unpredictable alarms and upheaval. Now it was clear that Ravelston was an equal and permanent partner in the scheme of things, a perception reinforced by the Governors' decision that new Technology Centres should be built both at Stewart's Melville and at The Mary Erskine School.

Both centres were designed by the newly-appointed Director of Technology, John Forth, but the impact on The Mary Erskine School was the more considerable. The Stewart's Melville project involved the adaptation and extension of an existing facility, but the Ravelston Centre, as it was formally called in celebration of the silver jubilee of the move from Queen Street, was a stunning combination of modernity and open-plan attractiveness. Overnight the school had moved into the very forefront of educational innovation. It was formally opened by Prince Philip, the Duke of Edinburgh, on December 13th 1991, the first recorded royal visit to the School in its long history.

The centre had actually been in use since August 1991, along with the Nursery and Preparatory classrooms of Easter Ravelston. Some hitherto junior classrooms now became available to the senior school, so that the Art, Geography, History and Modern Languages departments could be 'zoned' more effectively.

As if in response, girls flooded into the School to fill the extra spaces. The Senior School complement rose steadily from 560 in 1989 to 630 in 1993, reflecting the parental confidence exhibited by hundreds of respondents to an enormous questionnaire in 1990. The total number of girls in the Senior and Junior Schools as a whole was by now larger than at any earlier time, a startling commentary on the misplaced gloom of the 1970s.

This optimism found expression in an increase in the number of clans from four to six, Buchan and Lauriston being the names selected for the modern interlopers. The Governing Council also approved an increase in the number of teaching staff, in order to ensure that class sizes were attractive to parents. The Principal made a point of bringing on to the teaching roll a number of recently qualified teachers. This development, coinciding with the retirement of several senior teachers who had devoted decades of service to the school, ensured that the average age of the Mary Erskine staffroom became lower during the 1990s than in any previous period.

An era ended with the departure in June 1992 of May Burns and Kay Milligan, for they were the last teachers to have been on the Queen Street staff. Another reason for viewing June 1992 as a watershed was the retirement of the Deputy Principal and doughty champion of The Mary Erskine School, Eileen McCamley. The new Deputy Head, Norma Rolls, now led a management team consisting exclusively of married women, a point noted by Lydia Skinner, author of this book and Principal Teacher of History, who had retired at the end of the previous session. She too had taught at Queen Street, where she had been the prototype of the mother returning to teaching after raising her family. During her career at Ravelston, this had progressively become the norm.

The times were indeed changing. It was a less deferential society — styles of address between teaching staff became less formal, with Christian names replacing 'Mrs' and 'Miss' — and girls were encouraged, in part by their teachers and in part by a greater emphasis on oral involvement in English and Modern Languages, to become more forthcoming. The success of Sarah Crozier and Sarah Napuk in a national debating competition in 1993 was a reflection of such confidence.

Meanwhile, the School had tried to square its curricular circles. Technology was incorporated without loss to other subjects by the expedient of extending the working day and increasing the number of taught periods in each week, but this was part of a wider review of the curriculum, designed to ensure that girls and boys were fully equipped for future opportunity. They now began the study of their first Modern Language in Primary 4 and their second when they entered the Senior School. As Standard Grade curricula replaced Ordinary, the normal diet of subjects was increased from seven to eight, so that doors could be kept open for as long as possible.

Far from diminishing the quality of education, these expectations produced record-breaking results. By 1993, when the Scottish Office published tables of examination statistics, it could be seen that The Mary Erskine School's results at both Standard Grade

The Technology Department

and Higher were the best of all schools in Edinburgh. More girls entered degree courses in October 1993 than ever before, with the largest contingent going north to Aberdeen. The quality of academic education in the School received further affirmation two months later, when nine girls were awarded places by Oxford and Cambridge Universities.

If these achievements did nothing to dent the argument that girls fare best academically in a single-sex environment, there could be no doubt also of the continued value of twinning in the girls' broader education. In January 1992 the Carbisdale project achieved international recognition, through the award of the Ernst Enzensperger Prize for Outdoor Education, the first time that this Bavarian honour had been given to a non-German organisation. A few weeks later the two sixth forms came together for a special European Day, at which Otto von Habsburg was the main speaker. The Junior School was equally enterprising, inviting ministers and ambassadors from all the countries in the European Community to a conference at Queensferry Road during the Edinburgh Summit of 1992.

The arts flourished. Madalina Reed won first prize in the Scottish Independent Schools Art Competition in 1991. The twinned First Orchestra twice travelled to Prague — and Edinburgh marvelled twice at Czech virtuosity when these visits were returned. The Sixth Year Musicals mounted by Iain Scott and the two musical directors, Helen Mitchell and Roger Askew, became yearly more ambitious and accomplished; the 1994 production, celebrating the school's tercentenary, was the first performance of Peter Skellern's 'Poles Apart', written specially for the occasion and thoroughly topical in its Carbisdalean flavour. The school also commissioned a new work by Howard Blake, 'Land of

Counterpane', songs based on R.L. Stevenson's 'A Child's Garden of Verses', for a premiere performance by The Mary Erskine Choir in the Usher Hall.

If the Combined Cadet Force remained a quintessentially twinned activity, recruiting scores of girls each year into its ranks, sport was a medium through which girls and their teachers were able to display autonomous prowess. The tour of Australia by a hockey and tennis group in the summer of 1993 was the most ambitious project ever undertaken by any Merchant Company school.

1993 was notable also for foreign contact of a very different kind. In February, eight girls and three boys, all refugees displaced by the war in Bosnia, arrived at Edinburgh airport to begin a four-month stay, living with families and receiving full-time education at Stewart's Melville and The Mary Erskine School. The tears which were shed when they returned to their families in June were genuine indeed. The presence in the school of these spirited and courageous girls was a powerful reminder to the Merchant Maidens of 1994 not to take for granted their heritage or their civilisation.

Our story ends in 1994, with the celebration of the Tercentenary of the school and the announcement that this landmark in the history of Scotland's oldest girls' school would be marked by the visit of the Queen and Duke of Edinburgh. The Former Pupils' Guild adorned the school dining room with a wonderful ceramic mural by Margery Clinton. It consciously evoked the seventeenth-century Edinburgh herb garden which had been, in a sense, the source of Mary Erskine's fortune and her School's. Likewise, the kilt designed by Kinloch Anderson for the girls of the fourth century echoed the School's foundation,

Carbisdale

The Orchestra

Gymnastics

The Bosnian visitors

for its new Mary Erskine tartan was based on that of the Erskine clan with whom the school had been so closely associated throughout its existence.

1994 is an anniversary which, happily, can be celebrated by every one of the women and men who have led the School since 1945. All, in their very different ways, had been faithful to Mary Erskine's original vision, the provision of education specifically tailored to the needs of young women. As social attitudes evolved — from teaching girls to be women, through educating girls to compete in a man's world, to the current preparation of girls to be women in the modern world — it can be seen that the traumatic imposition of twinning had the ultimate effect of safeguarding Mary Erskine's legacy.

Given the turmoil and anxieties of the past fifty years, who can tell what the future will hold for this extraordinary foundation, which has changed sites and names so often and which has, through the continuity and tradition fostered by the Merchant Company, sunk such deep roots in the life and history of Edinburgh? The role of prophet can be left to the reader.

What this book reveals — and the current Principal recognises it with humility — is that Mary Erskine's School has been sustained above all by the patient service, dedication and love of a legion of unsung teachers, non-teaching staff and administrators, just as its history amounts to the faith of its parents and the character and achievements of its pupils. Every decade has posed its particular challenges. The family unbroken has met them with resolution, courage and tenacity — *Mitis et Fortis*!

The Founders of the Former Pupils' Guild.

APPENDIX

The Former Pupils' Guild

The text of this chapter was written by the late Anne Chalmers (Mrs.Wilson) for the 'Merchant Maiden' on the occasion of the Guild's centenary in 1984. It has been brought up to date by Audrey Lawrence, the current President of the Former Pupils' Guild.)

One evening in December 1884 a small group of young women met in the home of one of them at 57 Albany Street to form an Association which has grown, from those modest beginnings, to a membership of over two thousand scattered throughout the world. They rapidly set about appointing a Committee and declaring their aims. These were simple and straightforward and they reflect clearly their background and period. They aimed 'to encourage united work and a feeling of sympathy, to urge members to undertake a definite course of study .... and to inform of ways in which they can assist others'. The Edinburgh Educational Institution in Queen Street had been in existence for fourteen years; the idea of higher education for girls was novel and stimulating and it is not surprising that 'a definite course of study' to be pursued after schooldays was such a serious aim of those early former pupils. To launch their new Association, however, they sensibly organised a Social Meeting held, with the blessing of Dr.Pryde, their old Headmaster, in the School and this was encouragingly successful; people seemed delighted to meet again their old school friends and to dance and listen to music in 'the old dancing-room'. The Annual Social was soon an established and popular event and we are told that 'some amusements were introduced' — Capping Verses or a Spelling Bee, a recital by Dr.Pryde of his 'first poetical production' or a reading by Annie S. Swan of one of her own stories.

The intention had been to confine membership to those who had been pupils at the E.E.I. between 1870 and 1876, but the infant Guild found that 'it was in danger of dying of exclusiveness' and, with some misgivings, it opened its doors in 1891 to all who had attended the Edinburgh Ladies' College, as the Institution had been renamed. Not everyone thought that big was beautiful. Writing of the Social Meeting in 1893, the Secretary reports that it was attended by 'about 68 ladies'. Conscious that such vagueness might lay her open to some criticism, she goes on to explain that 'there were so many members present for the first time and not known to the Committee, that it was a little difficult to be certain, to one or two, of the number present'. One detects a sigh for the passing of the cosy days when everyone knew everyone else, but the Treasurer was probably happy at the thought of the potentially expanding membership; the early papers are full of references to the difficulty of extracting the annual shilling subscription.

It is not quite clear what happened to 'the definite course of study'. At one meeting in 1885, two members read papers on 'The Objects of the Guild' — both 'considered excellent'. The minutes record cryptically that 'Miss Todd's paper inclined to the theoretical side of the question and Miss Croal's to the practical'. Again, at a meeting in August of that year, there was a paper on 'A Comparison between the Elizabethan and Augustan Eras in English Literature', followed by a discussion on 'several literary and social questions'. Apparently only thirteen members came to that meeting, but this is charitably attributed to the 'inclement weather'.

However, as early as 1886 a Music Club was formed and a Reading Club and there were French and German Clubs by the end of the century. Activities Clubs have been formed over the years to meet the demands of members — for riding, tennis, badminton, folk-dancing — and have fallen away as demand fell. Others have taken their place. Today there are Clubs for Golf, Hockey and Swimming and members may join the Stewart's Melville F.P. Sailing Club and the Mercators Drama Club. There is also a Junior Section which organises its own functions and arranges badminton and tennis for those interested.

The Jubilee Dinner

No one may now meet to read essays on poetic subjects but in other ways our F.P.s are really remarkably similar to their forebears. Indeed, allowing for fashion changes, it is remarkable how enduring the patterns set by the early Guild have proved.

In addition to the Activities Clubs, based in Edinburgh, there are also Branch Clubs in other parts of Scotland and in England and for many years there were also Branches in British Columbia, Winnipeg and Melbourne. Today there are Branch Clubs in London, Glasgow, Manchester, Aberdeen, the Borders, Tayside and the West Midlands. The London Club was the earliest, being founded in 1920, and the West Midlands Club is the most recent, founded in 1980. In every case the object is the same: to provide a focus for friendship for Former Pupils living in the area, to provide a welcome to newcomers and to keep in touch with the parent Guild and the old School.

Very early on the Guild's founders realised the importance of keeping in touch with members, and from the first years a list of members has been maintained and circulated. For many years this was sent out as part of the Annual Report, which chronicled the Guild's activities in Edinburgh and outlined plans for the future. In our increasingly mobile society, this has become more and more difficult. Nowadays the two documents are separate; an annual leaflet or syllabus goes to all members everywhere, while a Membership List, painstakingly kept up to date, is reprinted every five years or so and still provides fascinating reading for those who want to follow the whereabouts of old classmates.

It was partly to maintain links between Former Pupils and between them and the School that the School Magazine, the 'Merchant Maiden', was started in 1908. This has a separate Former Pupil Section with reports of activities both in Edinburgh and the Branches as well as news of Former Pupils and contributions from them. Former Pupil readers can also enjoy the (much larger) section dealing with the present-day School, sighing with envy over the opportunities open to today's pupils and admiring their achievements.

Right from the start, the Guild, while keeping its own identity, has had very close links with the School. The founder members were encouraged and advised by Dr.Pryde, the then Headmaster, while one of the most dynamic Guild Presidents, in the early 1920s, Miss Mary Tweedie, herself became Headmistress a few years later. The Merchant Company too has always encouraged the Guild and valued its support, smoothing its path in the early days with permission to meet in the School building and, since 1922, with a Guild Room in the School where papers etc. are kept. There was also the valued privilege of using the Company's arms as a badge.

In return, the Guild has always sought to help and support the School, with many gifts over the years and with prizes. The earliest such prize was for Latin in 1895 and others followed, many from the Branch Clubs, either for merit or as a result of competitions — for example in singing, dancing and gymnastics. Perhaps the most valuable was the prize offered in 1935 to celebrate the Guild's Jubilee. This was a cash prize of £20 — sufficient at the time to pay the whole fees for a girl at the top of the School. Alas, even at its present enhanced value (and it now goes to two girls) it can do no more than help with some of the costs.

Gifts to the School — and many of these have also come from the Branch Clubs — range from money in 1913 to start a Branch Library, through the ceremonial table in the Hall (to mark the 250th anniversary of the School and the Guild's 60th anniversary) to the splendidly engraved glass entrance doors for the new School at Ravelston and an engraved goblet to commemorate the 350th anniversary of Mary Erskine's birth, the latter the work of Mrs.Alison Geissler, herself a distinguished Former Pupil.

The Guild deeply appreciates its links with the School and the feeling this gives of being part of the wider School community. Perhaps the most popular occasion of the year is the Summer Reunion at Ravelston, held in the Principal's splendid room in Ravelston House. The ladies of 1884 might raise their eyebrows at our Cheese and Wine, but they would certainly recognise the cheerful babble of chatter as old friends greet each other and catch up on news. Also well attended is the Annual Dinner in March, a more formal occasion and one of Miss Tweedie's innovations in 1922, when a very sumptuous menu cost ten shillings and sixpence. The Winter Coffee Morning attracts its own distinct group and there is always a faithful attendance at the Mary Erskine Service in June, held in Greyfriars where the first Merchant Maidens worshipped.

The Guild celebrated its Jubilee with a concentrated burst of activity in 1935. In the course of a few days they held a ball, a luncheon and a service of thanksgiving in St.Giles. Their successors marked their Centenary in 1984 with a series of events designed to involve as many members as possible and to strengthen the links with the School and the Merchant Company. These included the Annual Dinner, an Informal Evening in

Centenary Tea-party

The Heather Garden

Centenary Sampler

Gladstone's Land with a concert of music from Mary Erskine's day, a large attendance at the Founders' Day Service and the handing over by their President of the Heather Garden, the Guild's gift to the School. The Summer Reunion at Ravelston and the Mary Erskine Memorial Service at Greyfriars also attracted large numbers, as did a tea-party in the North British Hotel.

Some of the early Guild Clubs have died a natural death; these include the Sailing Club and the Mercators Drama Club as well as the Manchester and West Midland Clubs, while The Wine and Cheese Party has been replaced by a Lunch. However, Curling with D.S.M.C. and Aerobics are new options for Guild members. The School's Tercentenary in 1994 was marked by the Former Pupils' gift of a mural for the dining-room. Designed by Margery Clinton, it represents a herb-garden with the plants which would have been known to the School's Foundress, herself a herbalist and apothecary.

What would the ladies of 1884 think of their successors today? Surely they would be gratified that they had indeed become a Guild of Friendship which still held to the aims and spirit which had inspired their Albany Street meeting.

Dedication of the commemorative plaque at Erskine House, Queen Street

What the Well-Dressed Schoolgirl Was Wearing

Select Bibliography

Unpublished Sources

Minutes of the Merchant Maiden Hospital, 1856-1909 (M.M.H.M.)

Minutes of the Merchant Company Education Board, 1909-1990 (E.B.M.)

Accounts of the Merchant Maiden Hospital, 1860-1907

Register of Girls in the Merchant Maiden Hospital

Admissions Register of the School, 1870-1994

Teacher's Attendance Register, 1865-1870

Merchant Maiden Hospital Surgeon's Admission Book, 1849-1872

Petitions for Admissions to the Hospitals, 1894-

The Merchant Company Education Board; Abstract of Applications for Election to
the Foundationers of the Merchant Maiden Hospital, George Watson's Hospital
and Daniel Stewart's Hospital

Edinburgh Ladies' College Admission Registers, 1904-1912

The Edinburgh Institution Distinguished Visitors Book, 1871-

Edinburgh Ladies' College Leaving Certificate Examination Results, 1892-1898

Letter Book of David Pryde, 1870 (D.P.L.)

Letter Book of Robert Robertson, 1894-1912 (R.R.L.)

The 'Merchant Maiden' Committee Minutes, 1908-1909

The 'Merchant Maiden' by Eight Senior Pupils, 1908

The Company of Merchants of the City of Edinburgh,
Commemorative Material, various

Press Cutting Collections, various

Published Sources

R.D. Anderson, *Education and Opportunity in Victorian Scotland* (Oxford, 1983)

William Calder, *Outline of Lessons on the History of English Literature* (Edinburgh, 1895)

Mary G. Clarke, *A Short Life of Ninety Years* (Edinburgh, 1973)

The Edinburgh Merchant Company. Provisional Orders as to the Merchant Maiden Hospital, George Watson's Hospital, Daniel Stewart's Hospital and James Gillespie's Hospital and Free School (Edinburgh, 1882)

The Edinburgh Merchant Company. New Schemes as to the Hospitals (Edinburgh, 1889)

John Harrison, *The Company of Merchants of the City of Edinburgh and its Schools, 1684-1920* (Edinburgh, n.d.)

Alexander Heron, *The Merchant Company of Edinburgh, 1681-1902* (Edinburgh, 1903)

Bryan Lewis and John Robertson (eds.), *Stewart's Melville: The First Ten Years* (Edinburgh, 1983)

The 'Merchant Maiden', 1908-

Nancy H. Miller, *The Company of Merchants of the City of Edinburgh, 1681-1981* (Edinburgh, 1981)

Nancy H. Miller, *Peterhead and the Edinburgh Merchant Company. Visits by the Governors to their Buchan Estates, 1728-1987* (Aberdeen, 1989)

David Pryde, *Pleasant Memories of a Busy Life* (Edinburgh, 1893)

The Rules and Constitutions for Governing and Managing the Maiden Hospital, founded by the Company of Merchants and Mary Erskine in Anno 1695 (Edinburgh, dates various)

School Prospectuses

James Scotland, *The History of Scottish Education* (London, 1969)

Nigel Shepley, *Women of Independent Mind: St. George's School, Edinburgh, and the Campaign for Women's Education, 1888-1988* (Edinburgh, 1988)

Margaret Sommerville, *Mary Erskine or the Founding of the Merchant Maiden Hospital, now the Edinburgh Ladies' College. A Play* (Edinburgh, 1923)

Margaret Sommerville. *The Merchant Maiden Hospital of the City of Edinburgh, founded by the Company of Merchants and Mary Erskine* (Edinburgh, 1970; Oxford, 1993)

J. Thompson, *A History of Daniel Stewart's College, 1855-1955* (Edinburgh, 1971)

Index